FARMING BY INCHES;

OR,

"WITH BRAINS, SIR."

UNIFORM WITH

"MY TEN-ROD FARM."

by

Charles Barnard

LORING, Publisher,
319 WASHINGTON STREET,
BOSTON.

ROCKWELL & ROLLINS, Printers and Stereotypers,
122 Washington Street, Boston.

To Those,

WHO, NEEDING HELP,

WOULD HELP THEMSELVES,

IF THEY BUT KNEW THE WAY.

FARMING BY INCHES;

OR, WITH BRAINS, SIR.

CHAPTER I.

THE DREAM REALIZED.

"WELL, doctor, what is it?"

"Oh, nothing serious as yet. He seems very weak, but I cannot discover symptoms of any definite disease. I think his illness is more the result of overwork than of anything else. He is asleep now, and had best not be awakened." So saying he opened the front door and departed into the gas-lighted street.

Locking the door, I went upstairs, turned down the gas in my husband's sick room, and, wrapping a shawl about me sat down by the fire in the next room to watch and to think.

My husband, the head book-keeper in a down-town commission-house, had been brought home in a carriage that morning quite ill, He had not been well for some time, but, not thinking it anything serious, had continued his daily labor at his desk. At night he had seemed worse; so I called the doctor. You have just heard what he said as he went away a few moments since. We have been married about a year. This house, No. 95 Columbia Avenue, is our home. We are both orphans, and have no relations of any kind, save an uncle of my husband's living in Arenac, some fifty miles from the city. So far our married life has been very happy. Our income was sufficient to give us a home, comfortable, if not luxurious. But now a cloud had risen. My husband and bread-winner was sick, and that meant poverty. If he could not toil at his desk, our income was at an end, and with all our economy we had laid aside but a trifling sum for such a contingency as had now overtaken us. Should he remain ill for many weeks, our case would be desperate. Slowly turning over these things in my mind, I sat gazing at the fire, and trying to build up in the glowing coals some vision of the future. After a while, weary with watching, I fell asleep in my chair. Suddenly I seemed transported to some distant spot. I thought I was in a quiet room somewhere in the country. The window where I sat looked out upon meadows green, fair with flowers. Graceful vines trailed over the casement and cast a checkered shade on the floor. The sun was shining brightly, and a gentle breeze just stirred the leaves upon the tall trees that grew beside the house. Presently the door opened, and Robert, my husband, entered, and, oh, how changed! He seemed ten years younger. Perfect health flushed his cheek and sparkled in his eyes. His voice, usually so weak and thin, greeted me with loud and hearty welcome. Overcome with joy, I went to meet him — and woke up to find the fire out and the cold, gray light of a winter's morning streaming in at the window. Peering out through the frosted panes, I saw a heavily laden horse-car painfully toiling through the snowy street. A few pedestrians, well wrapped up, were hurrying along the sidewalk, trying to keep warm. The sky was the color of lead, and the air was full of falling snow. Altogether, it was a dreary scene. Going to my husband, I found him still asleep. As I stood looking at him, I was struck by the pinched and haggard expression of his face. It was the face of a man starved for the want of fresh air and sunshine. Presently he opened his eyes and smiled on me; but it only made me heart-sick to see it. It was a sad and weary smile.

But why prolong the story? For six long weeks I hardly left him for a moment. The doctor came nearly every day. My husband's employers called several times, offered every kindness, and, in the spirit of true and honorable merchants, continued his salary during his illness. At last he was able to sit up, and could even sit by the window for an hour or so, and amuse himself by looking on the busy street. Yet he seemed very weary and listless all the time. I tried hard, but failed, to interest him in anything. One day, to entertain him, I told him my dream.

"Yes, Harriet, but it was only a dream. Such a pleasant home is never destined to be ours."

Then he leaned back in his chair, and seemed lost in thought, while I went on with my sewing. In a moment or two a smile flitted over his face, and he stared very hard out of the window as if he saw something vastly amusing in the street. But this did not last long; he soon turned away, and the same old look of weariness returned.

"A penny for your thoughts, my dear," said I. "If they are pleasant ones, give me my share; if they are sad ones, let me divide the burden with you."

"I was thinking of your dream, and wishing we *could* make it come true. These brick walls and Farwell & Co.'s sunless cistern of a counting-room are slowly killing me. But it is of no use. I could not earn my salt in the country."

Farther conversation was then silenced by the entrance of the doctor. To tell the truth, I was not glad to see him. His bill was already large enough, and we should have a sorrowful time in paying it off, and to see it increased by another visit was not pleasing. Yet I was mistaken in the man. He had come to do us a real kindness. Going up to Robert, he took his hand and said, "This will be my last visit at present, Mr. Nelson. In a few days, I think you may venture out for a walk in the middle of the day. You must not think of returning to your desk for some time. To tell the truth, I have come this afternoon to say that in my opinion you had better never return to your counting-room at all. Nature has now given you one fair warning. This illness, if you read it rightly, is sent to inform you that she objects to your occupation. You must heed her, and give it up."

"Well, doctor, if I did not know you to be a man of sense and education, I should say you were getting quite wild. The thing is impossible. What can I do, if I leave the office?"

"That is more than I know; but I *do* know that you must throw up your business, or shorten your life by about twenty years. Your desk will as surely kill you as any other slow poison."

"You may be right," said my husband, after a pause. "I have even thought of this myself at times. But what can I do? Where and how can we live?"

"How you can live is more than I can tell. Where — is plain enough. You must live out of town — or die. Come, take my advice, sell out and move into the country."

"A very pretty idea, doctor; but in the country I should quietly starve. I may as well stagger along as I am for a few years, as to go from the city and die of poverty in a few weeks."

"Nonsense! man; you are sick, and hardly know what you are saying. The idea of a man of your education wanting for support anywhere! Take my advice, seek some out-of-door employment, — farming, surveying, — anything that will keep you out under the open sky and in the fresh air."

To this there was no reply save a gloomy shake of the head. Then the doctor bade us good-day. As I opened the door to let him out, he said to me, "Mrs. Nelson, there is but one thing to be done. Take your husband away from the city, and keep him away; that is, if you wish to see him live."

Next morning the letter-carrier brought a black-bordered letter for my husband. I gave it to him, and he broke the seal and read it. It did not seem to interest him much, for he merely said, "Old Uncle Jacob is dead. Poor man! his was a dull and lonely life up there at Arenac. It must be almost a relief to be taken away, and to join his long-dead wife and children." Then he continued his reading. Soon he came to something interesting, for he brightened up, and with a smile passed the letter to me.

It was as follows: —

"Arenac, *March* 3, 186-.

"Mr. Robert Nelson.

"Dear Sir: It is our painful duty to inform you that your uncle, Jacob Nelson, died at his residence a few days since, and was buried yesterday. We would have informed you of this before, but we were ignorant of the fact that he had any living relations. We were only apprised of it this morning by finding his will among his papers. By the said will you are made his sole heir. His property consists of the small house in which he lived, a parcel of land, and a small sum of money in our Savings Bank. The house is unoccupied at present, and awaits your disposal. The estate could be sold readily, if you have no other use for it. An early visit from you is desirable.

"Your obedient servants,

"CRESSWELL & JOHNSON,

"*Attorneys and Solicitors.*"

"When shall you go?" said I.

"Go where?"

"Why, to Arenac, to see our little estate!"

"No, I'll not go at all. I will write to these people, and have them sell the place and remit the money. I cannot afford the time or money to travel so far."

"Now, Robert, I object. Let us both go there. It will do us good to have a short trip into the country. The money will be well spent; besides, it will be but taking a dose of the doctor's last prescription."

At nine o'clock on the following Monday morning we were seated in the cars, ready to start for Arenac. There were but few seats occupied, and we arranged our wraps and shawls so as to have as comfortable a time as possible. Just as we had got nicely fixed, two stout countrymen came and sat down in the next seat behind us. They both took out papers and fell to reading. Soon we started. For the first half-hour we were speeding through the suburbs of the city. Then the houses dwindled away, and the open country with the fields and woods slid like a panorama past the windows. At first Robert discovered but little of interest outside of the car; but the sight of the brown fields and bare woods seemed to bring back memories of his boyhood, and he brightened up and manifested more signs of returning health than I had dared to hope for. After a while he became tired of gazing at the scenery, leaned back, and closed his eyes as if to rest, leaving me to my own devices. As for me I was only too happy to see him, as I fondly imagined, already getting better. Just then the two men behind us finished their reading and began to talk. They had evidently never learned the "car-whisper," and I could hear every word.

"How's business, Jack?"

"Good enough. We can sell all we can get. The trouble is to get enough to sell."

"What you selling, mostly?"

"Meat and sass. It is mighty hard work to get good sass up at Arenac. The farmers won't grow it, and we have to send to the city for all our stuff. Besides, the jobbers ask so much that our people won't pay us enough to make it an object."

"I found the same trouble at my place. They all want green sass in the spring, but don't want to pay such high prices. However, they will have it any way, and once a week I get up a car-load from town. I don't make anything on it. It is pretty well spoiled by the time I get it. I have asked Farmer Brown to raise me some; but he and all the rest do as their fathers did, and run in the same old rut. Any one who would raise sass for us would make a small fortune in time."

We reached our destination at noon, and went at once to the hotel. After dinner and a short rest, we started out to inspect the place. We found Arenac to be a manufacturing town on the banks of the Hoosensacken. The factories were all on the line of the river, and faced the single street that extended through the town. On the opposite side of the way were the various stores that supplied the material wants of the inhabitants. As we passed along the sidewalk, I saw one of the men who sat near us in the cars. He was standing at the door of the market, and seemed quite at home there. We found three hotels, and four churches, and these, together with the factories and dwelling-houses, made up a thriving New England village. A single covered bridge spanned the river near the railroad that crept along under the river-bank. Just over the river a lofty, wooded hill rose like a great wall, and lifted its rocky crags high over all.

The next morning we obtained the key, and started to walk out and see Uncle Jacob's little piece of property. We soon left the houses behind, and came to the open fields. The day was fair, and the March sun was shining brightly. The scenery, though brown and bare, was lovely. The walking was good, — and to walk or even live was a pleasure on such a day, — while the pure and bracing air inspired us with a sense of freedom and space to move about in, that was a delight only city-bred people like ourselves could appreciate. After passing several farms, we came to our own little place, as we had already learned to call it, though we never intended to occupy it. The house was quite small, — merely a one-story cottage, of five rooms. Behind the house was a small barn. The parcel of land we found to consist of a ploughed field, having thick woods on three sides, but open on the street, or south side. On entering the house we found it neatly but plainly furnished. Uncle Jacob had evidently been a man of refinement, if not of wealth. After inspecting everything, we sat down by the warm, sunny window to rest and admire the charming view. On the opposite side of the road, wide-spreading fields extended toward the village, whose tall spires and chimneys peered over the low hill beyond the fields. Beyond the village, Mount Arenac. To the right we could see far down the Hoosensacken valley, till the hills on either side were lost in the blue distance. To the left, thick woods.

"Charming view, — is it not?"

"Yes; but it must be very lonely here."

"That is true," said I; "yet I should enjoy living here during the summer months."

"And I, too. It would do me a world of good to spend a short time in this breezy mountain region."

"Why not do so? Why not shut up our city house, take a vacation, and stay here until the middle of April? By that time you will be so much better you can return to your desk with renewed strength and health. We can manage to picnic in this box of a house for a few weeks very comfortably. Then, too, we shall escape the raw east winds of the coast. It will do us both good, I am sure. Besides, it will be cheaper living here than at home, and the expense is something we have to consider just now."

Two days after this, our trunks were established for bureaus in our new residence, and my dream in a measure came true.

CHAPTER II.

FARMING ON PAPER.

As we intended to return in a short time we brought but little from the city, but used instead the things which we found in the house. Our time we passed in most delightful idleness. We had come for rest, and to recruit our health and strength; therefore we took things as easily as possible. We had but two meals a day, to save trouble. Most of the time we were out walking, or reading when the roads were bad. We slept a good deal, and did nothing a good deal more. About the twentieth of the month we began to recover our old-time health and spirits; for I found when the excitement of my husband's sickness was over, that I, too, was far from well. It was then I began to wish we could stay here all the time. Turning this over in my mind, I wondered what we could do for a support if we were to remain. We could not live in idleness, that was certain. At breakfast one morning, I opened the matter by saying: —

"What is sass, Robert?"

"Garden sauce, I suppose, — lettuce, beans, etc."

"Do you remember our first ride up to this place?"

"Yes; what of it?"

"Did you hear the conversation between the two men who sat behind us in the cars? Your eyes were closed at the time; perhaps you were sleeping."

"No, I was only dozing and heard every word. I have several times thought of what they said, and wondered why no one tried to supply their wants. I am almost tempted to do something of the kind myself; but I suppose we have not land enough."

"O Robert! do try it. We have a three-acre field. Is that not enough to experiment upon? Do try, please, for six months. Send word to Farwell & Co. that you have decided to give up your place; doubtless you can command another in the fall. It is of no consequence if we do not make anything by the operation. If we pay our way it will be enough. We can sell out in October, and return to the city with your health established for life."

"The idea, Harriet! The idea of our turning 'sass-farmers.' What could you do — a woman, or I — a book-keeper?"

"Do? Why, you can do anything, if you only try. The doctor said a man of your talents would prosper anywhere. As for me, I could help in many ways besides keeping the house, picking peas, washing lettuce, or other light work."

"What a woman you are, Harriet! With such a wife, a man would succeed in anything. I shall, I am sure. By the way, see what I found at one of the hotels yesterday."

So saying, he drew forth a small paper-covered book, — "Washburn's Amateur Cultivator's Guide to the Flower and Kitchen Garden."

"Just what we want," said I. "Fortune favors us slightly, Robert. Come, let us set up for 'sass-farmers' for a summer."

"Agreed! We will farm for a living for six months. Then we will cast our shells, and come out in our original characters as city-folks."

So far I have told my story as if I were the ruling spirit in the house. My husband's illness threw nearly all the responsibility of our action on me. As his health returned, I gladly gave up the reins, and henceforth this will be more the record of his doings than of mine, or, better, our doings, for in the new farming enterprise we had an equal share. I tried to carry out to the best of my ability the old-fashioned idea of a woman's being a helpmeet to her husband. At first I imagined in my ignorance that I could aid him directly about our little farm; but I soon found that there was an immense deal to be done aside from mere field-work. My share of the duties ultimately became that of house-keeper and accountant. In this I was fully employed. The house-keeping part was easy enough, but keeping accurate accounts of our sales and expenditures proved to be no small undertaking. After we were well under way hardly a day passed without its moneyed transaction to be attended to in detail. One day there would be a quantity of strawberries to be sent off, the bills made out, and the boxes accounted for; another day a wagon load of vegetables had to be counted, despatched, and properly accounted for on the return of the empty wagon. Perhaps you wonder why my husband did not see to this himself, he being a skilled accountant. It is true he could have done so; but every hour spent on work I could do as well was an hour lost on work I could not do at all.

Having fully made up our minds to try our hands at the business of farming, we resolved that all things should be conducted in the most systematic order. We would bring our methodical and mercantile ways of doing things into a business notoriously loose and inaccurate in its operations. Manifestly the first thing to be done was to draw up on paper some sort of a plan of what we proposed to do, and then endeavor to carry it out as nearly as may be.

After breakfast Robert walked to the village and procured the deed of our estate. Therein we found ourselves possessors of a certain parcel of land, bounded on the east by a line commencing on the county road at a stone post next adjoining the estate of Widow Comfort Jones, and running northerly three hundred and sixty-three feet, to the estate of Justin Stamford; thence westerly three hundred and forty-five feet, to the estate of Isaac Kempenfielder; thence southerly three hundred and sixty-three feet, to the county-road; thence easterly along said road to the first-named point, — the total area being one hundred and thirty-two thousand square feet, a little more than three acres. From this must be taken the land occupied by the buildings and the narrow strip of woods on the north and west sides. The woods on the east belonged to Mrs. Jones, "Widow Comfort," as she was called. After studying this over we walked out to inspect. It seemed very small on paper; but when we had walked over the frozen ground all around the bounds, we came to the conclusion that our little farm was quite an extensive affair when measured by feet and inches. At any rate, to go all round it was something of a walk. Little as we knew about such things we could not fail to see that, for our purposes, no place could be more favorably located. It was open to the sun all day, while the woods formed a shelter from the most troublesome winds. When we returned from our walk Robert got out writing materials, and, drawing a table up to the window, began to write, while I took my sewing and sat by his side, where I could look out far down the river-valley, and watch the shadows chasing each other over the distant hills. Presently Robert turned to me and said: —

"See, Harriet, here is a list of books on the subject of farming. I made it up from the last page of Washburn & Co.'s catalogue. I am going to the city this afternoon, and shall be gone two days. I shall get these books, and send them to you by mail to-night. While I am gone you can amuse yourself by looking them over, and finding out what there is in them that will be of use to us. We must follow the example of the students, and 'cram for a profession.'"

"Books, — I was thinking of them," said I; "but what is going to detain you in town so long?"

"Why, you see, if we really intend to turn farmers, the sooner we begin the better, and the sooner we cut all connection with the city the quicker we can commence. Here is a list of what furniture we shall need while here; the rest I propose to sell. I shall then pay all our bills, give up our house on Columbia Avenue, and dissolve my connection with Farwell & Co. Do you approve?"

"Yes, I like most of it. I approve of all your plans save the idea of leaving me here alone while you are gone. Why cannot I accompany you?"

"There is no reason why you cannot. But I thought to save you all trouble, and the pain of parting from our first home, besides the fatigue of the journey."

"I can bear the fatigue as well as you; and what if you should be taken ill, and I not near you? You are not yet a giant, sir, if you have lived in the country ten whole days."

At six o'clock that evening we were set down in the city. The street lamps were lighted, and as we went up town in a crowded horse-car, we could not fail to notice the difference between the sunny, quiet place we had left, and the dark, narrow, and noisy streets that hitherto we had thought perfection in their way.

The two following days were busy ones indeed. Finally, everything was accomplished, and we took our final departure from the city, bidding farewell, not without a pang, to our city friends and neighbors. They all thought our move a good one as a sanitary measure, but intellectually and socially — doubtful; financially — very doubtful. How far they were right in this, my story must unfold. That evening we lighted our new centre-table lamp, and sat down by ourselves in our own house, with thankful, hopeful hearts, and at peace with all the world. Every bill had been paid. We were under our own roof-tree, humble as it was, and about to embark upon a new enterprise, in which we could both have an equal share, and be to each other true helpers.

"Now, Harriet, let us draw up some sort of a plan of what we intend to do this summer. The first thing to be considered is finance. We have a house to live in, rent free. This furniture, together with that which is on the way to us, is sufficient for the summer. Our trunks contain enough for all our wants as far as clothing is concerned. The question now is, how much money must we have to support ourselves from now till the first of October? How much will it cost per month?"

"About seventy dollars," said I. "But shall we not receive a large part of our support from the farm? Will not the land contribute to our table?"

"Doubtless; but let us 'err on the safe side,' and go on the supposition that our farm is not going to pay anything. Then if it does not we shall not be disappointed, nor shall we suffer for want of a support. Seventy dollars a month for six months would amount to four hundred and twenty dollars. I propose to have this sum laid one side for this purpose. By so doing we can return to the city in the fall clear of debt, even though our farming speculation should prove a total failure. If the land does contribute to our dining-table, we will credit the farm with the value of the things so used."

"Why, Robert, you are going into farming like a banker. Do you propose to have a counting-room attached to the place, and to have huge ledgers wherein are entered every little item of receipt and expenditure, after the manner of Farwell & Co.?"

"Not exactly; but I do propose to apply mercantile precision to the pursuit of farming. See what a help it will be to us. If we make anything out of it, our books will show how to do it again; if we lose money, they will show us wherein we failed."

"I admit the advantage of all this; but will not the keeping of these accounts require a great deal of time and labor?"

"In the aggregate it will. Taking it up every day, and squaring the accounts each night, will reduce it to a very trifling affair. According to Uncle Jacob's will we have in the Arenac Savings Bank the sum of seven hundred and fifty dollars. The sale of our things in town, after paying our bills, produced two hundred dollars. Our own savings added to this make our available cash capital up to eleven hundred dollars. Taking from this, four hundred and twenty dollars for our support, we shall have remaining six hundred and eighty dollars for a working capital. Now, what shall we do with it in order to get the largest possible return? Let us consult our first agricultural friend, Washburn. Let us open the book at random, and see what we find."

So saying, Robert opened the book hap-hazard, and said, "Lettuce."

"Just the thing," said I. "Lettuce is classed as 'sass,'

and doubtless will sell well. Shall we put that down for one of our crops?"

"Yes; and having decided to try lettuce we must read up on the subject. Washburn says of it: —

"'The lettuce is generally divided into two classes, namely, cabbage lettuces and cos lettuces. The cabbage have round heads and broad-spreading leaves; the cos varieties have long heads and upright, oblong leaves.

"'*Culture.* — A very rich soil is necessary to produce fine head lettuce. Its crisp and tender quality depends very much on a luxuriant and vigorous growth. The earliest sowing may be made in February or March, under glass with slight heat. Keep the plants thin, and admit plenty of air to the frame every fine day. For later supplies, sow in the open ground as soon as the season will permit; transplant, or thin out the plants gradually to a foot apart, and keep well cultivated. The cos lettuces are excellent, if grown early in the spring, but run to seed quickly in hot weather. The large cabbage kinds are best, and most suitable for summer crops.

"'*Early-curled Silesia.* — Standard sort; very early; the best for forcing and the first spring sowing; makes a loose head; tender, and of excellent flavor.

"'*Early Tennisball.*— One of the oldest and most esteemed of the cabbage lettuce. The head is below medium size;

dark-green; very solid if grown in cool weather; one of the earliest and best.'

"And so on, for twenty or more sorts. All this is doubtless very fine, but I doubt if either you or I can understand it all. Wonder what a frame is?"

"I'm sure I don't know. The only frame I ever saw was a bonnet-frame."

Robert suddenly got up and went to the next room. If I had not known him well, I should have imagined he was offended at my levity. In a moment he returned, bringing two large books, which he laid on the table, saying:—

"I bought these yesterday. They cost a good deal, but as tools in our business they will prove invaluable. 'The American Gardener's Calendar,' by Bernard McMahon, and 'The Field and Garden Vegetables of America,' by Fearing Burr, Jr. You take one; I'll take the other, and we will read up on lettuce."

For the next half hour nothing was heard in the room save the slow turning of the leaves. Suddenly Robert shut his book with a slam, gave a low whistle, and said:—

"Goodness! What a tremendous thing lettuce is! I have read twenty-six pages on the subject, and am almost in a muddle over it."

"And my author refers to it on thirteen different pages. How shall we ever master the subject?"

"By perseverance and common sense. I am going to order some seed of Washburn this very night." Then he began to write a letter. While writing he went on talking. —"As far as I can understand the matter, lettuce seems to be something that can be forced; by that I suppose they mean it can be forced, or compelled, to grow in advance of the regular season by artificial means, such as shelter, etc. I cannot now tell how this is accomplished, but I have no doubt we can invent some method if we put our minds to it At any rate we will try."

The next morning the remainder of our furniture arrived from the city, and nearly the whole day was taken up in setting our new home in order. At nightfall we again sat down to our reading. To tell the truth, we were both fascinated with the books. Though we could not understand all they had to say, yet we found it a novel and pleasing sensation to read and talk about the real, tangible things of which they treated. We discussed lettuce far into the night.

I was awakened early the next morning by a great pounding in our barn. Hastily dressing, I went down to see what was going on. I found my husband had turned carpenter, and was busy with saw, hammer, and boards, making a huge box.

"What are you making, Robert?"

"A hot-bed frame. I made a lucky find this morning. In the barn chamber I discovered three sashes. I knew

what they were at once, and am going to make a frame to sow our lettuce-seed in."

"What a man you are, Robert! Where did you learn to be a carpenter, and who told you how to make a frame?"

"Taught myself—'Washburn.'" Then with a few finishing raps with the hammer, he stopped and said, "Come, let us have breakfast. I am as hungry as several bears."

"I am glad of it. It is a good sign, and shows that the doctor's prescription is beginning to work."

As we entered the house I glanced at the clock. "See, Robert," said I, "it is not yet six, and here we both are ready for breakfast. Such a wonderful thing never happened before."

After breakfast my husband took his hat and coat, and bade me good-morning, saying, "I am going to the village to procure some tools."

In about an hour I was startled by the sound of wheels in our yard. Looking out of the window I discovered Robert seated in an old hay-cart, and by his side a tall, elderly man, with iron-gray hair, blue eyes, and a face expressive of good-nature and good sense. As the team drew up at the door, I went out to meet them.

"My wife, Mr. Kempenfielder. Harriet, this is one of our near neighbors. I met him at the market, and he very kindly brought me and my luggage home in his hay-cart."

"Glad to see you, ma'am," said Mr. Kempenfielder, advancing and offering his huge, bony hand. I almost laughed when I took it, for I could not grasp such a digital immensity. He shook my hand, and at once I felt a new sensation. It was not like any in my experience. It was a hand-grasp expressive of honest, hearty, good-natured welcome. Not a "society" hand-shake.

"Glad to see you, ma'am. You're welcome to Arenac, I'm sure. Mary — she's my wife — was a-saying the other day she kinder wished some one would locate here. Old Jacob, he that lived here before, was a quiet man, and wan't very neighborly. He's your uncle maybe. Yes, I thought he was. Well, I'm glad you have come. Come over and see us when you get fixed. My folks will be mighty glad to see you. Hello! there, let me help you;" and away he went towards the hay-cart from which Robert was trying to lift a large sack full of potatoes.

"You aint very strong, are you? You look kinder peaked any way. Guess country living will build you up, soon."

So saying, he took the sack from the team easily enough. I could not fail to notice the man's great strength and Robert's weakness. Yet it did not disturb me. One was a farmer, the other a broken-down book-keeper. Which is the better man in other respects remains to be seen. Depositing the bag of potatoes on the ground, he then took several garden tools, rakes, shovels, etc., from the cart, and carefully placed them on the doorstep.

"Nice tools, those. Looks as if you meant to garden some."

"Just what we propose to do," said Robert. "We intend to run this small farm this summer."

"Do you though? Well, you are plucky. It's more'n I'd do, and I have farmed it for nigh on to forty years. You couldn't raise wheat enough on that to keep a man busy."

"We don't propose to raise wheat at all."

"Don't you though? Corn, per'aps?"

"No, we shall not attempt any heavy crops."

"What will you raise, — pigs?"

"We hardly know as yet, — not pigs, certainly. We may try lettuce."

"Lettuce! Raise lettuce! Well, I wish you joy in your undertaking."

So saying, he began to climb into his hay-cart. As he started off, he said he was glad to have us for neighbors, but guessed we had a tough road before us.

"Encouraging, — is it not?" said I, rather soberly.

"Yes — very —" said Robert, slowly; "but then if we

change our plans every time any one frowns upon them, we shall not get along very fast."

By noon that day Robert had placed his new hot-bed frame in a sheltered spot on the sunny side of the barn, and had placed the three glass sashes over it. As I went out to call him to dinner, I glanced into the frame, and found it nearly full of broken lumps of frozen soil. The sun shining through the glass was rapidly thawing and crumbling them to pieces.

"What are you trying to do, Robert?"

"Trying to thaw out a part of our farm. I placed those bits of frozen soil under the glass, and guessed they would soon melt. I have guessed right, it seems. By to-morrow I think we shall have some nice dry soil to sow our seeds in. But come, let us dine. After that we will go at our books again, and see if we can find out how many lettuce-plants we can raise. From all I gathered in the village this morning, I guess we can sell all we can produce."

This excited my curiosity, and as soon as we were fairly seated at the table, I asked for further information.

"The story is just this. I asked the man at the market if he ever bought lettuce in the spring. Yes, he did, large quantities. He could sell more if he was not obliged to transport it so far. This was too indefinite for me, so I asked what he meant by large quantities. 'Many dozens a day,' said he, and then he repeated his remark about the difficulty of obtaining it preventing still larger sales. As he seemed busy, I did not trouble him with further questions. Now, Harriet, let us rake up the little we do know about lettuce, and see what we can figure out of it. Do you remember what we used to pay for lettuce last spring?"

"About eight or ten cents."

"Well, if we paid, as consumers, eight cents, the provision store must have taken three cents for their profit, and the down-town 'Jobber' got three or more cents for his share, so that the grower only received about two cents per head. That seems a very small price; but let us reckon up what the grower could do with it as a crop."

Here my husband stopped suddenly, took out pencil and paper, and became deeply absorbed in some calculations. In a moment or so he looked up and said, "According to the books, lettuce must be planted one foot apart each way. Now, if I am not mistaken, one acre filled with plants one foot apart would contain forty-three thousand five hundred and sixty plants."

"Forty-three thousand plants? Goodness, Robert! How could we ever take care of such an immense number?"

Paying no attention to my remark he went on: "Forty-three thousand five hundred and sixty plants, at one cent each, would amount to four hundred and thirty-five dollars and sixty cents." Here he stopped abruptly, and began studying his figures again. As for me, I found something very interesting at the bottom of my tumbler.

"How much did you say it would cost us to live this summer, Harriet?"

"Four hundred and twenty dollars."

"Good. If we can raise an acre or more of lettuce, the question of our support for the next six months is nearly settled."

"Yes, if we *can;* but you must remember, so far we have been farming only on paper."

CHAPTER III.

THE BEST FERTILIZER — BRAINS.

After dinner Robert went out to look at his new frames, while I began to clear away the table. Before I had finished, he returned, bringing in a large sheet of rusty iron, on which was a pile of wet soil. This he gravely placed on the kitchen stove.

"What are you about, Robert?"

"About to apply caloric to a piece of our farm. The soil in the frames has melted, but is still too cold and wet, I fancy, to plant seeds in. I found this bit of Russia iron, and I am going to bake some of the soil on it until it is fit for use."

"Shall we have baked-farm for supper?" asked I, demurely.

"Yes, in time,—that is, we may have the final result of the baking for dinner or supper."

"But you have not soil enough there to fill a tenth part of the frames."

"I know it, my dear. I have a better idea than that. Wait a bit."

So saying, he went out leaving the pan of damp soil

on the stove. Presently, he returned, bringing an old raisin-box, some strawberry-boxes, and two or three cracked flower-pots. These he put down near the stove, and getting a seat and a book, drew himself close to the fire and began to read. The sight to me was simply funny.

"A pretty farmer you make, Robert! Toasting your toes and your farm there by the fire."

He never answered a word.

Looking out of the window soon after, I observed a huge four-horse wagon turning into our yard.

"Why, Robert, what is all this? What are these people bringing in here?"

"Manure, I suppose. I bought a large lot this morning."

Whereupon he took his hat and went out. In about half an hour I heard the empty wagon drive away, and my husband returned to his reading. The pile of soil had by this time begun to throw off a cloud of steam, and, drying rapidly, changed color from a disagreeable black to a rich, deep brown. Robert then took the boxes and pots and filled them all full from the heap of baked soil. This done, he placed them on the floor behind the stove and out of harm's way. Taking from his pocket a small package marked, "Seeds only," that had evidently come through the post-office, and opening it, he took out a quantity of small white seeds and carefully sprinkled them over the surface of the warm soil in the boxes and pots, and finished all by covering them carefully with more soil from the heap on the stove. Then throwing old newspapers over it, he stood contemplating his work. Suddenly, however, he started as if he had forgotten something.

"Oh! we must water them; but how shall we do it?"

"Take them to the sink and shake a wet brush over them," said I.

"A good idea, Harriet, seeing we have no watering-pot."

In a few moments this was done, and the pots and boxes were replaced on the floor with the papers over them.

The next day was Sunday. At the ringing of the second bell we stepped from our door into the warm and cheerful sunshine to walk to the village, proposing to attend one of its churches. We found the road filled with people, some walking and some riding, and all wending their way toward the village. Being city people, we walked rapidly at our usual sidewalk pace, and passed every one on the road. Soon we overtook a well-dressed lady walking soberly along by herself. As we came up with her, we ventured to speak to her.

"Can you tell us, madam, which is the Unitarian Church?"

"I can. It is the brown one with the tall steeple. I am going there myself, and will show you the way."

Thereupon we slackened our pace to keep in her company.

"It is a fine day, is it not?"

"Yes, the Lord adorns and gladdens his temple to-day. He delights to make it beautiful; but then, creation, his house, is always lovely. How fine the old mountain looks to-day, such charming light and shade!"

Not quite knowing what to make of this, I merely said, "Yes."

"Do you not admire the true and beautiful in nature?" continued our companion, turning upon us a face full of intelligence, serenity, and refinement.

"Yes," said my husband; "we do indeed. How can we help it with so much beauty spread around us this quiet Sabbath day?"

We had now reached the church-door, and our guide, whoever she was, passed in before us. Before she left us, however, she turned to say, "My own pew, unfortunately, is quite full to-day, or I would take you to it. But the sexton will, no doubt, find you seats. There he stands near the side-door. Good-morning."

"What a singular woman, Robert!"

"I hardly think that she belongs hereabouts."

"How so?"

"They told us, you know, we should find only boors in the country."

"They said so, to be sure; but it strikes me they knew nothing about it."

On our return from church, after service, we again overtook our friend just before reaching our own gate. She bowed and smiled, and we returned the salute as gracefully as we could.

"You must be the young people who have moved into the Nelson house?"

"Yes; we have come to spend the summer here for the benefit of our health."

"You could not do a wiser thing. Free air and sunshine are cheap but wonderful remedies for every ill, mental or bodily."

"Do you live near us, may we inquire?"

"Yes, I am your next neighbor. Comfort, — Comfort Jones is my name."

"I am quite pleased to know it," said my husband, extending his hand. "Let us hope to see more of you, Mrs. Jones."

"Thank you, sir. But you must remember, I am an old and very quiet person. I do not venture out much, and am simple and plain in all my ways; not in the least like the gay people you have left in the city."

"Quiet simplicity is what we desire, madam. My wife and I know how to appreciate it, I assure you."

"Indeed we do," said I. "None are more simple in their tastes than we."

In truth, this sweet-faced, self-possessed old lady quite charmed me.

"I hope we shall see more of you, Mrs. Jones."

"You shall;" and she bade us good-morning and disappeared in the woods.

We had a very early breakfast the next morning, as Robert said he had a great deal of work on hand. Breakfast over, he put on stout leather boots and a suit of old clothes, and went out to meet two laboring men who arrived from the village at seven o'clock. I saw no more of him till twelve, when he came in to dinner. We had changed our dinner-time since removing to Arenac, and dined at the unromantic hour of noon. This we found divided our day much more evenly than one or two o'clock. Indeed, one of the first surprises of our country life was the extraordinary length of the days. In town we breakfasted at eight, and had tea at six; but now the daylight seemed to be several hours longer, and an earlier breakfast and later tea required our dinner to come at noon. After dinner Robert brought a large quantity of potatoes into the kitchen, saying, as he did so: —

"Can you not help me a little, Harriet?"

"With pleasure."

"I want these potatoes cut, so that I can plant them."

"Plant them? How can you? The ground is still frozen hard."

Without a word he went to the next room, and procuring a book opened it and pointed out a paragraph. I read it.

"So you intend to force potatoes."

"I mean to try something of the kind. I have no hot-bed; but as it is nearly April, I am going to attempt 'forcing' by the aid of the sun alone."

"But can you do it?"

"I don't know. I can try it, and find out."

"A good idea," said I, seizing a potato, and preparing to cut it in two.

"Wait a bit. We don't know how to cut our potatoes yet. Let us see what the books say on the subject."

"Precisely."

Then my husband read, as follows: —

"'Cut each root into two; three, or more pieces, according to the size, minding, particularly, that each piece be furnished with one or more buds or eyes.'"

In an hour I returned to my sewing, having finished the potatoes. During the greater part of the day, heavy teams, loaded with manure, had been toiling through our gate and out upon the open field behind the house. After supper, I asked Robert what he proposed to do with so much material.

"Spread it on the land, and have it ploughed in as soon as the spring opens."

"But will it not be a very expensive operation?"

"To be sure. But, then, 'Nothing venture, nothing have.' I expect to spend three hundred dollars in manure alone."

"Three hundred dollars? Why, that is nearly half of our whole capital!"

"I know, my dear. But, without this expenditure, we can effect little or nothing."

"That may be true, but how are we to buy horses, ploughs, cultivators, carts, and all else to work with, if the manure costs so much?"

"I propose to do without them. We may come to own a horse by and by; but it will not be for our farm-work."

"How, then, do you propose to cultivate your crops?"

"By hand. You remember our trip to New York?"

"Remember it! Shall we ever forget it? It was our —"

"And do you recollect standing on the deck of the steamer, as we swept toward Hurl-Gate, in East River."

"Yes."

"Well, you know I pointed out to you on the shore, near the outer limits of the city, one of those little half-acre market-gardens, filled solid with growing crops, the plants standing so closely together that they fairly touched each other, and hid the very ground from sight?"

"Oh! yes. And how beautiful they were with their squares of different shades of green! And, do you remember, sir, the headache you had soon after, and how I had to play nurse for the first time in my life?"

"Indeed, I do. And a charming headache it was, or, rather, nursing, I forget which. Now, I hope to conduct our little farm as those Dutchmen do their gardens. I mean to pack our crops so thickly on the land that there will be no room for horse or plough. In short, my plan is to 'farm by inches, and by hand.'"

When I came downstairs the next morning, I found my husband very intently studying the boxes and pots of seeds which he had placed behind the stove, and, on looking at them, I found them covered with myriads of small green plants just thrusting themselves through the soil.

"See, Hattie, what heat, moisture, and darkness have done. They have forced these seeds to germinate in three days. But now we must move them into the light and air, or we shall soon lose them." Upon which he took them all up, and placed them near the window, in the sun, saying,

"After breakfast, I must move them to the frames in the yard."

"Well, Robert, pray tell me how it happens that you know so much about such things. When and where did you study botany?"

"I will answer your question by asking you another. I graduated at Harvard, did I not?"

"Yes."

"Well, that will account for everything."

After breakfast, the plants were removed to the now dry and warm frames. The soil in them had been worked over and raked smooth, and looked very fine and nice. The boxes of seeds were placed on the soil, under the glass, and in one of the empty frames. Robert now proceeded to plant the potatoes I had cut up the day before. Opening a narrow trench with his hand, he packed the bits of potato, cut-side down, as thickly as they could stand, just like herring in a box, then another row, and so on. When it was finished, the soil was smoothed over them, and they were plentifully watered from a watering-pot Robert had bought for the purpose. There were thirty-five rows, and eighteen in a row, making in all seven hundred and thirty "sets," as the books called them. The few potatoes that remained were carefully washed and — eaten.

By this time the weather had become warmer, and the

frost was out of the ground. The next day, the third of April, was so mild and pleasant that I went out after breakfast to see what was going on. I found the entire field behind the house dotted over with small black heaps of manure, and two men at work spreading it thickly over the ground. Seeing Robert over by the woods with a yoke of oxen and a man holding a plough, I went toward them to watch their operations. Before going many steps I discovered the whole team approaching me. Taking a good stand I waited to witness the procession. First came a pair of sturdy oxen; then Robert, glorious in big boots and a mighty whip; next a huge plough tearing its way through the soil; and lastly, Mr. Kempenfielder. Immensely entertained with the performance, I took out my handkerchief and cheered them on. They never took the slightest notice of me (at least Mr. K. and the oxen did not), but went sailing away and left me alone in the middle of the field. I put up my handkerchief, and started for home. But seeing them soon at a stop, I turned toward them.

"Well, Robert Nelson, I never expected to see you driving a pair of oxen."

"No more did I. It is my first attempt. Mr. Kempenfielder showed me how to drive them, and there you see the result."

"The straightest furrow I ever seen drawed," said Farmer K. "I don't see how he did it."

"My army experience taught me that. When I was Sergeant of Co. 'F,' 190th Mass., I very quickly learned to draw a straight line across an open field by simply 'alligning' two distant objects." Taking out his watch Robert looked at it and exclaimed, "Why, it's ten o'clock! I had no idea the sun was so high. Please, Hattie, go and look at the lettuce-plants. If the thermometer in the frame stands at 70°, or higher, lift up the back of the sash, and put a stone or something else under it to let the surplus heat out."

On going to the frame, I found the glass covered with steam. Looking at the thermometer I found it at 90°, while the plants seemed to be beaded with dew. Lifting up the back of the sash I propped it up about an inch with a bit of stick. Opening the sash where the potatoes were I found everything steaming hot; but as Robert had said nothing about opening it, I let it remain as it was, and went into the house. At noon Robert came in and said I should have aired the potatoes. The heat had wilted them badly. So much for ignorance. He also said I must go out at about four o'clock, and let the sash down again to shut the heat in for the night; which I accordingly did.

At six o'clock I went out to call my husband in to supper. I found him near the barn talking with Mr. Kempenfielder, who was preparing to go home after his day's work.

"It's a mighty heavy dressing you have put on your land, Mr. Nelson. I never seen the like in my life. It must have cost you a sight of money."

"It was a costly operation. But an extra heavy dressing will give an extra heavy return, I suppose. At any rate, it will not be my fault if the land does not yield her increase. In addition to all this barn-manure I shall put on about a hundred dollars' worth of superphosphates, lime, ground bone, and guano."

"A hundred dollars' worth! why, man, you're crazy. Who ever heard of such a thing?"

"I have, — or, rather, I have read of it in the papers. I think I have seen somewhere that the gardeners around New York sometimes put six hundred dollars' worth of fertilizers on one acre of their land."

"Perhaps they do. Them that has money can afford to throw it away in that fashion."

"I cannot positively say whether they can afford it or not. But I do know they keep throwing it away year after year, and I don't imagine they do it for amusement."

"I have heard tell of them fellows; but I don't believe

mor'n half that's told of 'em. One of them came and settled round here a few years ago and tried sass-raising, just as you proposed; but, then, he was a poor shote of a fellow, and his farm soon drank him up, or he it, I don't remember exactly which. Besides you have a kind of manure which he did not have. He used plenty of the barn-stuff, but you seem to use more yet, and in addition put on to your land a better manure still, — brains."

CHAPTER IV.

SEED-TIME.

Two days after this Mr. Kempenfielder had completed the ploughing and harrowing, and he and the laborers went away. In their stead Robert hired a lad from the village to work for us during the summer. He found a boarding-place near by, and was to be employed on our farm all and every day, Sundays excepted. After tea, on the day the ploughing was finished, we walked out to inspect, and to make up our minds where we should place our various crops. Our land consisted of a single unbroken field, with the house and barn placed near the road in the centre. Directly through the centre a path or road-way had been laid out from the barn to the woods in the rear. This gave easy access to all parts of the place without wasting much space. All the remainder of the land had been thickly spread with manure and ploughed one way. Then it had been cross-ploughed in the opposite direction, and after being harrowed again and again the soil was reduced to a fine level surface. Little as we knew of such matters we could not fail to notice the thorough manner in which the work had been done.

"What other crops than potatoes do you intend to plant?"

"I hardly know as yet. We must consult Washburn & Co., and the books. I have thought a good deal about it the past two days, and have been tempted to write to Washburn & Co. for advice. For my own part I have no preference. Our only object is to raise such crops as will give us the greatest money return. If it pays best to raise radishes, we will do so. If we find more money in string-beans, we will establish a monster beanery at once."

"For my part, I think it would be best to consult the market-man. You hope to sell your crops to him, and he can tell just what is most in demand."

"Good! Harriet! I'll go down and see him to-night, so that we can order the seeds by to-morrow morning's mail. Despatch is the word, — I'll go at once."

So saying, he went toward the house, and I saw no more of him until nine o'clock. The order for the seeds was written and duly mailed early the next day. Soon after breakfast it began to rain. As little or nothing could be done out-of-doors, Robert set our new boy — Jack by name — to work cleaning up the barn, and on returning to the house we both gave ourselves up to the study of our books. Reading and talking about our new profession filled up the entire morning. After dinner we again went at the books, and among other things we came to the subject of transplanting, or removing growing plants from one place to another.

"Must not those lettuce-plants be transplanted by and by?"

"Yes; they will have to be transplanted twice, if we may believe the books. Once into the frames, and after that from the frames to the ground. This would be a good day to do it. I wonder if I had better not do it this afternoon. We may not have another cloudy day for some time."

"What! go out in all this rain?"

"To be sure. Why not? I can put on an old suit that the rain will not injure."

"It is not for the clothes I fear, but for you. The only result will be a severe cold, and perhaps a return of your illness."

"I do not fear that in the least. I will dress warm and not stay out long. If I feel the slightest chill I will come in at once."

Thereupon he put on an old hat and coat and went out to get Jack to help him. As for me I was very uneasy at the whole proceeding; but my fears were groundless it afterwards proved. A short time after this I went to the kitchen window to see if they had yet finished their undertaking, and I saw my husband and Jack gravely planting out the lettuce, and the rain pouring from their clothes in little streams. Vexed at Robert's foolhardiness, I rapped on the window and beckoned to him to come in. All the reply I got was a very wet smile and shake of the head. Quite provoked at what seemed mere folly, I returned to the dining-room and sat down in no pleasant frame of mind. Soon after I heard him come in and go upstairs. In a few moments he came down fresh, cheerful, and dry.

"No harm as yet, Hattie. Nor do I fear any, We planted both frames nearly full. We put them one inch apart each way, which gives us about three thousand five hundred plants. It took only a small portion of our plants. We have several thousand more in the boxes and pots."

To my surprise, no harm ever came of this venturesome proceeding. In time I learned to see my husband go out in all weather with complacency. Rain or shine, it made no difference; he never felt any ill effects from the exposure. Perhaps you will wonder at this. The only explanation I can give is, that a warmly clad person at work in the open air is too much occupied to stop to think about taking cold. Imagination goes a great way sometimes.

That night, thanks to the promptitude of Washburn & Co., a large package of seeds came to us by express, and we spent the evening in examining them, and in making ourselves acquainted with their different methods of culture.

The following is a list of the contents of the package:—

Beans.	Cucumbers.	Turnips.
Beets.	Peas.	
Cabbages.	Radishes.	

Now it is impossible for me to give you a detailed account of all our doings. Sufficient is it to say that as soon as the warm weather opened, about the 15th of April, we went to work at our planting. I say we, for I was so much interested in all that was going on that I could not stay in the house, but, putting on a short dress, I joined Robert and his boy Jack in the field. We had had several showers and the soil was beaten down hard by the rain. At Jack's suggestion the ground was loosened with a hoe and then raked smooth.

As I told you before, the farm was divided into two parts by the narrow roadway or path. This path extended north and south, and at the upper or northern end, next the woods, our first planting operations were begun. The first thing we took was beans, — string or bush beans, — the early yellow six weeks and early Mohawk. These were the two sorts we selected from Washburn & Co.'s catalogue. Jack took the hoe and began to break up the soil; Robert taking a rake went after him raking it all smooth, while I held the seeds and performed the part of "the admiring spectator." But this did not suit me. I could not be idle while others worked; so, as soon as a slight furrow had been drawn with the hoe, I began to drop the seeds about two inches apart, as the books directed.

"Wait a bit; we must not forget the phosphates. Jack,

get a wheelbarrow and bring one of those barrels that stand in the barn."

Accordingly the superphosphate was brought and thinly scattered in the furrow or drill. When about half way up the first row I stopped. A new idea had come to me.

"Are you sure, Robert, that you have placed these rows in the right direction? Ought they to run north and south parallel to the road, or east and west at right angles with it?"

"I can't see that it makes any difference. The sun shines down between the rows, and they do not shade each other, if they are placed north and south. However, I suppose they will grow as well one way as another."

"That is not what I was thinking of. Suppose now your beanery was all up and in bearing order, and you wanted to gather a few bushels for market; will it not be very awkward to have to walk with a heavy basket half-way down one end of the plantation, then turn at right-angles, and go up between the rows in order to get to the centre of the field? You certainly cannot go stepping over the rows. That would be still more awkward. Now, it seems to me, if the rows were placed the other way, you could go to any spot you wished by the most direct route."

"Harriet you are — a — well, you are everything that's nice. Come, Jack, stop there. We will carry out her idea and turn our plantation round end-ways. Never mind the beans that are planted."

So we began again. Jack prepared the ground, Robert put in the fertilizer, and I placed the seed. After planting several rows I left them and went to the house to prepare dinner. As I passed the lettuce-frame I looked at it. The young plants were growing rapidly, and had stretched themselves up so that they covered the soil from view. Altogether it made a very pretty sight, — green, fresh, and thrifty. To my surprise I found the potatoes had sprouted and were growing finely. As I looked at them, I wondered how we were ever to get them out. They seemed to have quite grown together. While I was setting the table for dinner I happened to see Washburn's "Guide" on the table. "Let us see, — did I not read something about bush beans there? Oh! I fear we have made a mistake." At that moment Robert came in.

"What day of the month is this?"

"The sixteenth."

"Do you call this the middle of spring?"

"I should say not. It is early spring yet."

"Read this: 'All varieties of beans are very sensitive to the frost and cold, and should not be planted before the middle of spring.'"

Without a word he laid down the book, and, taking up

"Burr on Vegetables," dived into it with the greatest eagerness. After turning over the leaves for a moment or two he closed the book and opened McMahon's.

"What are you looking for," said I.

"Some crop that will stand the frost and that can be planted early. We must be doing something if we are blocked at the outset. If we ought not to plant beans, we can try something else. Ah! I have it, — peas. Come, let us dine."

After dinner we went out to make a new start in the planting business. Marking off a large square having an area of about half an acre we began again. Having planted one row, Jack commenced to prepare another about three feet from the first.

"Hold on, Jack, — that won't do. We must not waste our land in that fashion. Make the rows nearer together."

Jack dissented from this. "Nobody ever planted nigher than three feet. Farmer Stamford, and Farmer So-and-so never planted less than three feet."

"Perhaps he is right," said I.

"Perhaps he is, and perhaps he is not. How much manure does Farmer Stamford put on his land?"

"Oh! a lot, — as much as ten one-horse loads to an acre."

"Ten loads to an acre! There are fifty loads here,

besides the superphosphates and other fertilizers. You may make the next row eighteen inches from the last. There is my foot rule. We will measure the space off by inches."

We worked hard till six o'clock, and had the satisfaction of seeing our "pea-patch" nearly planted. While at the tea-table I was surprised to find the bread and butter disappearing very rapidly.

"Why, Robert, what is the matter? I never saw you eat so much."

"Eat so much! It is you that are doing the eating. I am quite ashamed to see that you have eaten so heartily."

"Well, I was hungry."

"So was I."

Upon which we had a good laugh at each other. Our out-door work had given us both wonderful appetites.

"We are very unfashionable, my dear."

"To be sure we are, but good health is unfashionable also."

The next day was a real April day. Clouds, sunshine, and showers, delightfully mixed. I did not venture out myself. Robert and the lad finished the peas before we had much rain, and at about ten, I heard them at work near the lettuce-frame. Throwing on a waterproof I went out to see what was going on. Jack was holding a large flat basket, while Robert was carefully prying up the potato sets with a flat stick. He was obliged to be very careful, as the small shoots that had started from the eyes were very tender and brittle. At first many of them were broken in handling; but he soon learned to dig them up without injury. When the bottom of the basket was covered they started for the field, and I after them. First the boy stirred up the soil, then my husband opened the ground with his hands, scattered a little guano through the soil, and taking one of the potato-plants carefully set it in the ground, leaving the green tips just showing through the soil. As for me, I carried the basket. In about two hours we had finished the work, leaving the plants three feet apart each way.

Several showers passed over while we were busy, but we let it rain. For my own part, I rather liked it. It was a novel sensation to be out in the rain with no umbrella. What would our city friends have said if they had seen us? It is true, my dress became fearfully soiled; but it was an old affair and could be easily washed. Just as we were going to dinner I looked back over the newly planted field. It seemed very thinly occupied, and appeared wasteful as far as space was concerned.

"Can we not grow something between the potatoes, Robert? Is there not something that will come to maturity before these plants cover the ground?"

"Just what I was thinking of. We will consult the books after dinner."

But the books did not help us, and we were thrown back on our own resources.

"How would beets do?"

"Not at all. It would take so long for them to come to maturity, that the two crops would crowd each other and become mixed up in inextricable confusion."

"You don't understand me. I mean beets as beet-tops, not as roots."

"Oh! ah! I see what you mean. Sow the seeds thickly between the potatoes, and then pull them up and sell them when the tops are young and tender. Sell them for greens."

"Precisely."

"Well, Harriet, all I can say is, that you will make a capital farmer if you keep on. Where did you acquire so much brightness?"

"Caught it—just as one would the measles—from my husband."

That evening we had a call from our neighbor, Mrs. Jones. She proved to be a lady of good sense and education, and well acquainted with the best literature of the day. We were both vastly entertained by her visit. She had views of her own on all subjects of interest. Art, music, and politics were familiar matters with her. Among other things we touched upon our farming operations.

"I have heard of your doings. It has made a good deal of talk in the village already. They all seem to think you will make a wretched failure of it. I tell them to wait. It is not the first time a city-bred man has tried farming. Many have done so, and succeeded too, which is more than can be said of some regular farmers. You intend to confine yourselves to garden crops, I hear."

"Yes. It is purely an experiment with us. We only intend staying for a few months, and while here we follow the business of gardening for a support."

"I am glad to hear it. I should really like to see some such active young people as you are make the experiment, and then give us the result. Perhaps you could settle the vexed question, Does farming pay?"

"If we fail in every other respect we can at least do that. We can show by our books just what it does cost, and ascertain how much profit there is in it."

"I am glad to hear you say this. Farming, as carried on about here, is a haphazard affair. They never seem to know precisely where they do stand, whether they are making or losing money. Can I help you in any way? My husband when he was alive was a skilled gardener, though he did not follow it as a profession. I wish he had. He might have lived to this day instead of grinding his years away over his desk."

"Thank you, Mrs. Jones. Doubtless you can help us. For our own parts, we know little or nothing beyond what we have acquired from books."

"Books! — what do you want more? Books, with brains, and I fancy you can both furnish them, will accomplish anything. I have quite a library of agricultural books. I shall be happy to loan them to you at any time."

"Thank you, we shall be delighted to avail ourselves of your kindness."

"That is right. I sometimes fancy that books love to be read by people who appreciate them. Come and see me to-morrow evening, and I will place my whole library at your disposal. It will be a pleasure to see my books once more in use."

The next day opened fair, but soon clouded over and remained so the rest of the day. Robert at once took advantage of the shade afforded by the clouds to plant out the lettuce-plants. I did not assist him about it, but went out once during the morning to see how they prospered. As we were determined to use every foot of our land, it was a matter of importance not to waste any by planting too far apart. To make sure of having the young lettuce-plants stand just twelve inches apart, Robert made a marker, as he called it. I called it "Nelson's Patent Lettuce-planter." It was simply a ten-foot strip of board, having small pointed wooden pegs fastened to it every twelve inches. By holding this over the soil and letting it fall, ten small holes were made in the soft earth. Into these the roots of the plants were dropped, and with a slight pressure of the fingers they were fastened upright in the ground. The planter was then used again, and so on. After trying it a few times they became quite expert, and when I came out to see them they were setting out the plants at the rate of three a minute. When I again went out, to call Robert in to dinner, the entire three thousand five hundred had been set out, and they had begun again on the lot of plants that were still growing in the pots and boxes. But here they met with a difficulty. The plants were growing so close together that on pulling them apart they were found to be drawn up very thin and weak.

"So much for not knowing that they should be planted out in a frame to give them more room, and make them stocky. They quite starved each other, and are valueless. We are a long way behind our forty-three thousand plants, Harriet."

"I know it; but can we not try again? Can we not sow more seed, and transplant them before they are too old?"

" I do not know, I'm sure. We can but try it."

After dinner, Robert prepared a new bed in the frame, and sowed lettuce-seed all over the soil. This he did to force the plants along, intending to plant them out in the field as soon as they were large enough. About half-past five I went out once more to inspect things. The frame had again been planted with lettuce, and all the spare land between the young potato-plants had been raked over, and beet-seed thinly scattered and raked in. I found the two people at the farther end of the place preparing to make another plantation.

" What do you propose to put here, Robert?"

" Turnips."

" Why, I thought they were only useful as a late crop,— planted in the fall for winter use."

" So they are; but do you not remember seeing small bunches of white turnips in the market, at home, in June?"

" Yes; we used to pay a shilling a bunch, and were glad to get them at that price."

" Just so; it is that shilling which has induced me to try turnips as a spring crop."

" A good idea; but, come, supper is ready."

As we walked slowly along the path toward the house we passed the new lettuce plantation.

"Is that not a waste of room, Robert? Can you not grow something between those plants?"

"Now, Hattie, you are going too far. That is carrying things to a pretty fine point. There are only twelve inches between the rows now. In thirty days the lettuce-plants will touch each other."

"Perhaps so; but is there not some small quick-growing crop we could get off before the lettuce reaches that point?"

"I am sure I cannot think of anything, and I doubt if you can."

"Don't be so sure, sir. Wait till I can consult our books."

On reaching the house I examined "Burr on Vegetables." After a short search, I found these words: "If space is limited, radishes may be sown with onions or lettuce."

CHAPTER V.

WHAT IT DID COST.

THE following evening we called on our new friend and neighbor. As we walked up the gravelled path, and approached the little cottage where Mistress Comfort lived, quiet strains from a reed organ, skilfully played, greeted our ears. The door was opened for us by Comfort herself, who looked and spoke a comfortable, cordial welcome. If we had been surprised to hear the music in such an out-of-the-way place, we were still more astonished and delighted on entering the brightly lighted parlor. A two-banked organ, pictures, books, comfortable furniture, and a glorious open wood-fire. Could any city parlor furnish more? And the lady of the house, — did she just step from a glass case, or is this all a dream?

"You seem surprised."

"We are, madam. We thought country people were — well — not like this — rural."

"You must have got your ideas of the country from the opera, — pretty but ignorant shepherdesses, gay with ribbons; or from story-books, — the men bowed down by labor, and the women only capable of gossip and bad grammar."

"For our own part we were ignorant. Others told us that on leaving the city we should bid farewell to all that makes life endurable; that dwellers in the country never rose above the clods in which they delved, or had an idea beyond cows and such things. If one may judge from the specimens the country sometimes furnished the city, they were not so far wrong."

"It is true, a portion of the agricultural community are so weighed down by toil that they seem but little above their own cattle; yet, for all that, you will find, in a given number of country people, just as much virtue, refinement, and education as in the same number of city people in the same circumstances in life; no more and no less. The only difference I can see between the town and country is, that in the country there are no very poor, no very rich. Human nature is the same everywhere."

We had quite a lively debate on this point, after which conversation branched off to other matters. A more delightful evening we never passed. Our host exhibited her pictures, played for us, and lastly loaded us with books to take home and examine at our leisure. As we rose to go, Robert said:—

"Please, Mrs. Jones, may I ask one more question? How happens it that you prefer living in this retired spot, when your wealth and tastes would so naturally lead you to the city, among all the advantages of concerts, lectures, and society?"

"Simply because I am not wealthy. A little money goes a great ways in the country. The cost of living would be so much greater in the city that all my income would be expended on my support; that is, such a support as I should desire. Here the cost is so much less that I can indulge, as you see."

This set Robert thinking, and all the way home he was as quiet as a mouse.

The next day the planting was resumed, and by the first of May all was finished, save the beans and cucumbers; these we left until some time after. Would you like to view the result of my husband's labor? Come and see. The day is mild and bright, the ground dry and clean. Birds sing in the air, and a green mist seems to float in the woods. The grass by the roadside is bright and fresh. Far down the valley the river sparkles in the sun, while the hills, marked off in various patterns, show where the fields are planted with varied crops, and every crop a different shade of green; blue sky and flashing water; purple mists on the far-away hills; a hundred shades of green on every hand, and over all a flood of light. Now for details. As we go up the path extending through our little farm, the first thing we see is a long, narrow bed, or border, reaching from the path to the fence. It is four feet wide, and one hundred and seventy-five feet long. Thickly dotted over it are thousands of delicate leaves just breaking through the moist soil. This is Robert's seed-bed. The plants are cabbages. By and by they will be carefully transplanted to some other place. Next we come to a broad strip of land, covered with solid ranks of peas, about three inches high, thrifty and vigorous. Here are our thirty-five hundred lettuce-plants growing rapidly, while between every row a narrow thread of green shows where our radish-plants are hastening to maturity. Beyond these is another and larger lot of lettuce. These are quite small, having been planted later than the others. There are about ten thousand little plants dotted at equal distances over the ground. The same delicate thread of radish extends between the rows of plants as in the other lot. Here is our turnip-field looking finely. The rows are very thickly filled with plants, but Jack is busy thinning them out by hand. He has two boys to help him, for it is no small job. Every plant has to be examined; the weak ones pulled out, and those that are to remain left standing about four inches apart. There is half an acre of plants, — at least twenty thousand. If we get half a cent apiece for the turnips, this little plantation will yield us one hundred dollars; so you see, as far as money is concerned, our farm already presents a cheerful aspect.

Beyond the turnips are the early potatoes, and among them the reddish-green leaves of the beets are spreading over the ground, and filling all the spare room. Lastly, is the empty space where we began to plant the beans. They never came up at all. On digging a few up to see what was the matter, we found the seed quite mouldy and dead. We had lost our labor and the seed by planting too early. The spring rains having beaten the soil down hard, Robert and Mr. Kempenfielder are at work upon it with a horse and light plough. Mr. Kempenfielder is leading the horse, and Robert holds the plough. They have stopped to turn at the end of the field.

"You have held a plough before, aint you?"

"Never touched one before," said Robert.

"You can't tell me that. You hold it as if you had done so a year."

"Do I? It is only because I imitated you as nearly as I could. This is my first lesson in ploughing."

"Then you beat all I ever see. My boy Tom took mor'n a month to learn to plough."

"How so? Was he not a bright boy?"

"Bright as a dollar; but somehow he never could seem to give his mind to it. He was always a-reading books and wanting to go to sea."

"Did you let him go?"

"Yes. It went agin us, but his mother and me finally give in, and he went. He never would have been contented on the old place. He said it was too lonesome and there was too much work about it. He wasn't far wrong there. Farming is dreadful hard work, and no mistake. You'll find it so, I reckon, before you get through the summer."

"I have not found the labor very severe as yet; but then my farming is quite different from yours. Come, start up your horse. We have no time to lose;" and away they go, horse, plough, and all.

In about an hour the work was finished, and the whole team came slowly down the path, just as the factory whistle blew long and loud for dinner. As they passed the lettuce-beds Mr. Kempenfielder stopped and asked what they were.

"Lettuce and radishes."

"You don't say. All them lettuce? What can you do with such an everlasting lot of them?"

"I hope to sell them."

"And what do you expect to get?"

"A cent a head."

"Only a cent. Why there aint more than eight or nine hundred all told. That won't bring you much."

"It would not be a great deal if there were but nine hundred. According to my counting there are over thirteen thousand plants in that lot."

"Thirteen thousand! Why, at a cent that would be over a hundred dollars. A hundred dollars off that pocket-handkerchief piece of land!"

"That is the way I figure it. Besides the lettuce, I hope to get a bushel or two of radishes off that same ground."

"Radishes! Where are they? I don't see 'em."

"Right before you, between the lettuce-plants."

"What, them little things? Lor! I thought they was weeds. Well, well, it's a kind of farming I could not follow. I should have to wear my specs all the time to see the crops. A hundred dollars off that place; but after all, it must have cost a sight to raise 'em."

"It did cost something, but not a hundred dollars by any means."

Now, perhaps you, like Mr. Kempenfielder, would really like to know what it did cost,— how much money my husband has sunk in our operation thus far. Seeds have been bought, manure has been spread with a lavish hand, and the labor must have cost something. I myself became a little uneasy to see the money go so fast, and one evening, about the first of June, we sat down to make an examination of our ledger. Robert had not been so careless as to go blindly on spending money without a thought. I found he had the whole thing at his tongue's end and knew to a cent just where we stood.

THE FARM, DR.,	June 1.
To two hundred loads manure	$200 00
" guano, ground bone, etc.	100 00
" ploughing	15 00
" labor	10 00
" two months' labor of boy	50 00
" seed	10 00
" incidentals, tools, etc.	15 00
	$400 00

Four hundred dollars so far. No return as yet. In addition to this we must enter our support for that time, but we will leave this till we come to the final summing up of our affairs in October. My husband's labor should also be added to the cost of our farm; but that, too, we will defer for the present. Whether we shall receive enough from the place to pay him for his toil remains to be seen; however, the prospect is cheerful.

CHAPTER VI.

OUR FIRST HARVEST.

With the advent of June came the first real, downright, hard work, — weeding. It was a novel experience with us city people, to discover the charmingly independent way the weeds had of coming up at all times and in all places. Little did they care for our pet lettuce, or beloved radishes. They (the weeds) came up seemingly in a night, and in the very place they were least welcome. In fact, they were not welcome at all. As soon as they made their appearance we went forth to receive them with all honors. Getting our tools, we started out "like an army with banners" (hoes), and made a vigorous attack on the first we met. They were among the young cabbage-plants in the seed-bed. We very quickly found our hoes were quite useless here. The only thing to be done was to carefully pull them out from between the plants. After a while I was obliged to give it up and beat a retreat to the house, leaving Robert and the boy to finish the undertaking. The labor was quite beyond me, requiring more endurance than I could command. Just before noon the seed-bed was finished. At dinner-time Robert came in, looking tired, flushed, and hot. In a few moments he was ready to come to the table, having washed and dressed for dinner. This is something he never omitted. If he did farm for a living, there was no occasion for his sinking the gentleman. He did not follow the example of some of our farming neighbors, and come to the table in his shirt-sleeves, but maintained the same habits he acquired in the city. Promptly at one o'clock the work was resumed. As soon as I had finished clearing away the table I went out to see how they prospered. To my surprise I found them at work among our newly planted beans. I had supposed they would take things in order.

"What induced you to skip over so many things, Robert? Why did you not take the peas next?"

"Beans must not be hoed when they are wet, — makes them rust. They are dry now."

"Who told you so much?"

"Books." And he rapidly plied his hoe, throwing in the words between the sharp ring of his tool, as it slid over the ground, gently stirring the surface and setting the young weeds adrift. The sun was shining brightly, and the weeds as they lay scattered about on the warm soil soon wilted away in the heat. Just where they were at work the soil was fresh and brown beneath them, a few feet behind it changed color, and a yard or two back it was quite dry and dusty. This to me seemed very singular. I did not know that the soil would part with its moisture so quickly. While thinking about this, a new idea came to me. Is there not a better tool, and a quicker way of doing this work? The hoe Robert is using is only six inches wide, and each stroke tears up a strip of weeds the width of the blade. Would not some other tool do the work as well, and in half the time? Without a word I went back to the barn, and procured a light iron rake. Selecting a spot where the weeds were pretty thick, though very small, I began to draw the rake back and forth over the ground, as if for my own amusement. After going a rod or so I threw it down, and went over to where Robert was at work, near the fence. As I approached I discovered that Robert and the boy were not alone. There was a man, a farmer apparently, and a stranger, leaning on the fence and talking with Robert.

"It must have cost you a sight to have fixed things up as slick as you have here?"

"Certainly it did," said Robert, still swinging his hoe and talking at the same time. "It has cost several hundred dollars already."

"Several hundred dollars! You must have plenty of stamps to be throwing them away in that sort of way."

"If I supposed I was throwing money away, I would stop at once, and not spend another cent."

"You'd better stop any way. Farmin' never did pay,

and I don't believe it ever will. The more land a man has, the poorer he is off."

"The first part of your proposition I doubt, the last part I can understand readily. If I were obliged to cultivate a hundred acres I would give up at once, and turn to some other occupation."

"I've got two hundred on my place. Its the old Stamford farm, next door. My father left it to me, and I've managed to starve on it all my life, and my children too,— that is, what's left of them. The boys ran away; the girls can't, so they don't. They is willing enough, I dare say. Well, I don't blame 'em. Farmin' is a dog's life, and mighty poor pay, unless perhaps a fellow has lots of capital."

"There is one kind of capital you have as much of as anybody."

"What's that?"

"Time! All the while you have been standing there leaning against the fence, doing nothing, I have hoed a whole row of beans, and have thereby added to their value at least fifty cents."

Finding the conversation becoming pointed I went back to examine the result of my labor. Just as I supposed, the rake tore the weeds out of the ground, and the sun quickly killed them. I cannot see but that the work is as well done as with a hoe, and better in one respect.

"Robert, please come here and bring your hoe. If you have a foot-rule, please measure the blade of your hoe, and then measure my rake."

"I have no rule, but can place them side by side and compare the width of each."

Taking up the tools he laid them side by side.

"The rake is more than twice as wide as the hoe; if the hoe is six inches, the rake is more than twelve. I see what you are aiming at, Harriet. You think the rake will do twice as much work as the hoe; that every stroke will go over a greater space, and consequently there will be a saving of time and labor. A good idea, but will it work? Will it do as well? Can you kill the weeds by raking them up?"

"Come and see."

"I declare, Hattie, that is a success. How came you to think of it?"

"Pure inspiration. Country living has clarified my brain. I shall expect to shine" —

Looking up, I discovered that the man by the fence had climbed over, and was standing near, with his hands in his pockets, staring open-mouthed at our doings, and saying: —

"I swaney if she aint got a head-piece. Who'd a-thought it would work so? Every weed's killed. I don't believe Sally or Jane would have done it."

"Hallo, Mr. Stamford!" said Robert, "where did you come from? I was afraid I had driven you off. This is Mr. Justin Stamford, Harriet, our next neighbor through the woods."

"Glad to see you, ma'am. You is the first lady I ever see that showed a spark of interest in farmin'."

I returned the salutation as well as I could, being somewhat amused at the queer mixing up of heads and rakes.

Taking up the rake, Robert went to work, raking the weeds instead of hoeing them, leaving me to entertain Mr. Stamford. This I was not inclined to do. It was nearly four o'clock in the afternoon, — high time all reasonable people should be about some regular employment. Yet here was this man, idly stopping to talk; and talk he did, in a straight line, till I could stand it no longer; so, as politely as I could, I escaped to the house, much wondering at the man's utter indifference to the value of time. Perhaps he is a man of property and leisure, thought I. He don't look it, and he says he has a two-hundred-acre farm. How is it possible he can have any leisure at this time of the year and with such an estate?

So the days sped away and the summer was at hand. Our days were devoted to the farm, and our evenings to reading for profit or pleasure. We read all the agricultural books we could obtain from our neighbor, Comfort, besides taking the "Cultivator and Country Gentleman," the "New England Farmer," and other rural papers. In these we found a vast fund of valuable information. We could not understand it all at first, but after a while we learned the meaning of the technical terms, and then it was easy enough. The only thing that troubled us seriously in our reading was the immense number of details and minute directions for doing things, and, what is more, every writer seemed to have a pet method of his own, and gravely informed the reader that his way was the only one to be followed. As we oftentimes found a dozen articles upon a given subject, and all proposing a different style of doing a thing, it was somewhat embarrassing.

"What shall we do, Robert? One man says, do it my way; another says, no, my way is the best; and a third offers still another plan. They all say they have each tried their own method, and succeeded also. How can that be?"

"They are all more or less right. There may be several ways of performing some agricultural operation, and each having some one point of advantage over the other. All we can do is to select the method which seems the most simple and the nearest to common sense."

Here is a list of a few of the books we read: —

"The Field and Garden Vegetables of America," by Fearing Burr; a useful and valuable book.

"The American Gardener's Calendar," by Bernard McMahon. This had the operations of each month placed together, — a great convenience. The only trouble with the book is that it attempts too much, and confuses the novice.

"The Elements of Agriculture," by Geo. E. Waring; a scientific work, but plainly written, so that it can be understood by any one of ordinary education.

"The Chemistry of the Farm and Sea," by J. R. Nichols; full of information, but, for all that, not a book which would aid us greatly. We did not spend much time over it.

"The Field-Book of Manures; or, the American Muck Book;" by D. J. Browne, stuffed with information like a chicken ready for dinner, and, like some stuffed meats, requiring brain-sauce and salt to go with it.

"A Manual of Agriculture," by George B. Emerson, and Charles L. Flint. This we found to be a school-book; as we were not above going to school, it helped us wonderfully after we had found time to master it. During our first experience at farming we gained but little from it, as it required study to understand it all.

"The American Home Garden," by Alexander Watson; a useful and sensible book. Yet to read it one must have some knowledge of gardening beforehand. Not having it, we could not avail ourselves of the book till some time after we began business as "sass farmers."

These all and many others we read as carefully as we could, and gathered from them what help we needed. At that time Henderson's "Gardening for Profit" was not published. If it had been, we could have saved ourselves many mistakes.

About the first of June Robert started off one morning for the village, "to buy a team," as he said. About noon I heard some one drive into the yard, and on going to the door I found Robert, with an animal, — a horse they called it, ancient and bony. On the creature's back was a light harness, whole, but decidedly old. Behind the beast was a small open wagon with one seat. If the horse looked old the wagon seemed older still.

"How do you like my team, Harriet? Lovely creature, is he not? His neck is not 'clothed with the thunder,' but it has a good collar on. The valley does not tremble 'when he paweth it;' and when he 'smelleth the battle afar' he don't say a word; yet he can drag a load of potatoes, to say nothing of lettuce, and he'll do."

"How can you talk so, Robert? What did you buy such an establishment for? I am sure I shall never ride in such a thing."

"It is not for our riding that I got it, but to carry our crops to market. The day of our prosperity is approaching, and you can tell any of our city friends you write to that we now keep a horse — and cart. How much do you think I paid for my team?"

"I am sure I don't know."

"Just fifty dollars for the wagon, horse, and harness. It will carry our crops to market, and we can sell it when we return to the city, if we ever do so."

"Do you think there is any doubt about our return?"

"Yes; my health is so much better since I have lived in the open air that I am half inclined to stay out under the sky for the rest of my days."

"How about our support in that event?"

"That is a question I imagine this rickety old wagon will soon settle."

It did settle it in a measure the very next day. Just about daybreak the next morning Robert started off to market for the first time. He returned in time for a late breakfast, and as he rose to go to his work he placed a blank book and a small roll of bills in my hand, saying, as he did so, "Our first sales, Hattie."

3 bushels of beet-tops, at 75c.	$2 25
12 doz. lettuce, 50c.	6 00
6 " bunches of radishes, $1 00	6 00
1 bbl. of peas	8 00
	$22 25

That evening Robert was late to tea, so I went out to see why he did not come. I found him by the barn, with a huge pile of radishes before him on a rude bench. He and the boy were busy tying them up in bunches of ten each.

"Slow work, is it not?" said I, taking up a few, and preparing to make up a bunch myself.

"Yes, it is very slow. At this rate we shall have to hire more help soon in order to gather our crops. The peas are rapidly ripening, and the lettuce is all heading up at once."

"How would it do to employ girls about your picking?"

"I don't know. I never thought of it."

"It would be worth trying, at any rate."

"Do you think we could find any girls to work for us, Jack?"

"Can't say, sir. Never heard tell of such a thing before."

"Can you not ask Mr. Kempenfielder, or Mrs. Comfort? Perhaps they could help us," said I, tying my bunch with a piece of string. Just then a new idea came to me: Is there not some better way of doing this?

"Would we not save time if we divided the labor, Robert?"

"How so?"

"Why, you make up a bunch, while I get the string and tie it when you are ready."

"A good idea; only you must not use twine. Take some of that Russia matting soaking in the water-pail. Twine would cut the roots, and injure their looks and sale. The matting is soft and easy to work with while it is wet. When it becomes dry, it shrinks, and holds the bunch tightly in place."

Robert then made up the bunches, and I tied, as he held them. By so doing, we got on twice as fast as before.

"Still another idea, Robert. Suppose, instead of your flesh and blood fingers, we had some wooden ones."

Without waiting to even thank me for the suggestion, he dropped the radishes, and went into the barn, and I soon heard him at work with hammer and nails. In a few minutes he returned, bringing a small wooden rack, or frame, looking like a reduced saw-horse. Placing it on the bench, he threw a few radishes into it and tied them up in an instant.

"You place them, and I will tie them."

Soon we had quite a pile of bunches before us.

"Lend a hand, Jack. Take them away and wash them, while we tie them up."

At the sight of our improved method the lad opened his eyes very wide, and said: —

"See what larnin' will do. Goodness! If I had sich a head-piece as that, I wouldn't be the poor devil I am."

Robert was up at daylight the next morning as the team was not quite ready for market. He and Jack worked hard, and at half-past five Robert drove out of the yard with his wagon piled up with boxes and barrels. After breakfast I entered the following in my account-book: —

20 doz. lettuce, at 50c.	$10 00
15 " bunches radishes, at 80c.	12 00
1 bbl. peas	5 00
1 bush. beet-tops	50
	$27 50

After dinner we both walked over to neighbor Kempenfielder's, to see if we could get any helpers to work for us on our place. As we approached the house, we caught sight of a far from charming picture. There stood Mr. K. in his shirt-sleeves, and at his heels were three unruly children, screaming and making themselves generally disagreeable. At the windows were two girls, about ten and twelve years old, while a boy was chopping wood near the door. Two dogs, a cat with several kittens, seven cows and a calf, also assisted in the tableau. The house, a large, old-fashioned affair, was flanked on one side by a huge barn, with its door idly swinging in the wind, and on the other by a rickety shed, filled with all sorts of carts, wagons, and tools in various stages of decay. All around the garden was a low stone wall, decidedly dilapidated, literally one stone falling from another. Though the day was warm, every window in the house was closed, and as we entered, it was like going into a musty garret. The lady of the house, fat and forty, if not fair, opened the door and ushered us into the best room, crowded with uncomfortable furniture placed with mathematical precision about the room, and drawing up the curtain let in enough light to make things visible. After the children had been quieted and sent out of the room, Mrs. Kempenfielder opened matters by remarking on the weather and crops. From this the conversation slid to our doings on our own little farm.

"We are very busy just now picking peas," said my husband; "we have so many, and as the price rules high, we are in search of pickers."

"Labor is plenty enough," replied Mrs. K. "My husband had lots of it offered to him; but we don't keep but two men. It is as much as your life is worth to get their pay out of the place, to say nothing of anything more."

"Indeed! I supposed you kept at least ten or twelve men on such a large farm as this."

"Ten or twelve men! Lor, bless you, no! Who could stan' it? Two's bad enough."

Just then, Mr. K. entered. He had procured a coat, and

was plainly ill at ease in it, or in the room, I don't know which. Evidently the parlor was for show and company.

"It is labor you are looking for, — is it? Plenty of it round, such as it is, — Irishmen and Germans."

"We are not in want of men at all. We want young people, — would prefer girls."

"Girls! girls to work on your place?"

"Certainly. The work is light and not difficult."

"I never heard of such a thing before. Girls work on a farm! — not much. It would kill 'em right off. A girl or woman might as well hold the moon as a plough. You nor I will never see such a thing as a woman at work out-of-doors, and, what is more, I hope we never shall. My daughters never will, at any rate."

"You know, sir, a great deal more about farming than I do; but I cannot see what objection there can be if a girl or woman assists about a farm, — picking peas, tying up turnips, gathering strawberries, or any occupation requiring a quick eye and ready fingers. There are hundreds of young girls, daughters of poor men, who would gladly earn something for their own support if they could know how, and were not afraid of Mrs. Grundy."

"Who is Mrs. Grundy?"

"The old lady who lives next door, and always says 'They say,'" said I, coming to the rescue.

"You don't mean Mrs. Stamford," said Mrs. K., firing up suddenly.

"Oh, dear, no. Mrs. Grundy is not a woman at all, or rather she is all women."

This puzzled her mightily, and she relapsed into silence.

"Perhaps you are right, Mr. Nelson, yet I fear you will not find what you want about here. None of the native girls would come down to such work. They'd be glad enough to get the money, but the working for it would stop 'em sure."

Finding we were to get no assistance, Robert turned the conversation to other matters, and after a while we bade them good-afternoon and walked on toward the next house, just beyond the woods.

"What an unlovely home!"

"Yes, and what a life! It is not living at all; it is mere existence."

"Vegetating."

"Well said, Harriet. Those people haven't an idea above potatoes. Oh, if that is farming, may I never be a farmer! I don't wonder the son ran away."

"But need farm life to be so sunk in toil and ignorance?"

"I am sure I do not know. Perhaps these people we are coming to can tell us. I suppose this must be the Stamford place;" for we found ourselves standing before a small cottage house with a pretty flower-garden by the front door. On either hand wide-spreading meadows lay warm and fair in the afternoon sun, the breeze just stirring the tall grass and waving grain. A noble great barn stood behind the house, and everything betokened neatness, order, and substantial comfort.

"What a splendid farm!" said Robert.

"And what a charming home!"

"Let us go in, by all means;" and we did.

Mr. Stamford was a-field, but his wife and two daughters welcomed us kindly. We found them to be pleasant and well-informed people, without a trace of rusticity. This surprised us, as we supposed, from what we had seen of Mr. S., that his family would be oppressively rural. The true explanation of this came out afterward. Among other things mentioned during our visit was the matter of "pickers."

"Just the thing!" exclaimed the elder of the young ladies. "Why should not girls work out-of-doors in the fresh air and sunshine? I am sure I wish I could."

"Father would never let you, Jane," said the younger. "He and mother attend to everything, and do not let us do anything about the house or farm. It is nothing but mend and sew, sew and mend with us; or it is read, read, read, all day long, till we have read every book and paper we can find. I wish father would work less and read more, and let us work more and read less."

"Hush, Sally!" said Mrs. Stamford, reprovingly. "Your father, as you well know, grants every reasonable wish you have."

"Yes, mother, all except the very reasonable desire for some regular employment."

"How can you talk so before Mr. and Mrs. Nelson? Doubtless they quite agree with your father."

"To tell the plain truth," said Robert, "we do not agree with him at all."

Fortunately, just at this point, Mr. Stamford himself entered the room, and the conversation was diverted to other channels. In a few minutes, however, it wandered back again.

"Perhaps you could work girls on your place if you had 'em, but I dunno where you'd find 'em."

"I would go in a minute if I were not — were not — so far advanced in years," said Jane.

"So would I," said Sally.

"Come, girls, do talk sense or not at all," broke in Mr. Stamford, testily.

Seeing rocks ahead, and fearing a wreck, Robert skilfully steered one side, and sailed away on another tack.

When we left Mr. Stamford's, we went home by the way of Mrs. Jones'. As we passed her house she beckoned us in, and while there we mentioned the employment matter. The idea seemed to strike her favorably, though she confessed she could not help us about it. At last she brightened up, and said she saw a way out of our difficulties, — advertise.

The next evening, the "Arenac Plaindealer" contained the following: —

"Wanted, at once. A few smart, active girls to work in a market-garden. The labor is light, and the pay reasonable. Apply to

"ROBERT NELSON, *Upper Road.*"

CHAPTER VII.

OUR LEDGER.

THE next day but one we had a queer commentary on Messrs. Kempenfielder and Stamford's ideas of female labor, by finding twenty-one girls and sixteen boys paraded in our yard, all eager to obtain the "light work, and reasonable pay." The boys we rejected at once. Why they came at all is more than I know; perhaps they were modest, and thought they could do a girl's work. Selecting six of the brightest-looking girls, we dismissed the rest, and they went back to the village sadly disappointed. Our six pickers were soon introduced to the "pea-patch," and, as we were quite as ignorant as they as to the best method of picking peas, we let them help themselves about it. However, they were bright, and quickly learned that the true way was for each to take a row, and pick clean as they went. We paid them by the bushel, and thereby induced a lively competition, which resulted in our mutual benefit. After they had gleaned the peas, Robert set them to work tying up turnips, in bunches of four each. Jack pulled the roots, trimmed the tops, and brought them to the girls in the barn, who, after tying them, washed and packed them in boxes for market.

Robert took a full load to market the next morning. He did not return as soon as usual.

"Had to find a market this morning, Harriet. Our store would not take my whole load, so I drove round to the other stores; however, I sold out, and there is the account and the money": —

4 bbls. of peas, at $4 00	$16 00
25 doz. lettuce, at 12c.	3 00
6 " bunches radishes, at 75c.	4 50
20 " " turnips, at 37c.	7 40
	$30 90

The six girls we retained in our service several days, and then, as the rush of work was over, discharged four of them, keeping two for a while longer. The four who were sent away were sorry to leave. The two who remained worked rapidly and well, and seemed to enjoy their occupation. Part of the work would be considered by many very dirty. Neither we nor the girls thought so. A pile of turnips covered with earth is not a lovely sight, and to handle them seems very disagreeable; yet good common loam is not dirty; it washes off easily and leaves neither stain nor smell. I have tied up many a bundle of radishes and turnips, yet my hands will compare favorably with those of any lady in the land.

The two girls took to their work kindly. They even offered to do that which we did not expect of them. They perfectly gloried in pushing a rake over the ground after a shower; and when it came to setting out the cabbage-plants, after the peas were gone, they took hold of that, and beat Robert and Jack in the quickness and neatness with which they set out the young plants. The girls stayed with us about a month, and during that time gave entire satisfaction. When they left us we found that they had improved wonderfully in health and strength, and as they went away, I could not help remarking that they were two of the most robust and hearty girls I had ever seen. To be sure, they were very much sunburned, and rejoiced in freckles; but I have yet to learn that a sun-tanned face is a disgrace, or that freckles are a bar to happiness. So much for the girls; now for the outside effect.

The fact of our employing female labor in our market-garden produced a perfect uproar in the place. It set the whole town by the ears; indeed, we did not know before that two such quiet people as we could create such an excitement. A few praised our actions, but the greater number of the people condemned us in unmeasured terms. "The Arenac Plaindealer" approved of our doings, and thought we had performed a good work, in showing a new field for the labor of girls and women. "The Arenac Bombarder" lectured us severely, and wrote slashing articles after the manner of those newspapers which are just a little behind the age, and very conservative.. Nothing was too bad to be said of our disgraceful proceedings. "The reign of fanaticism had begun. The radicals had invaded the village. Society would soon be subverted, and the government overthrown." As for ourselves, we employed the girls as long as we wished, and discharged them when it was convenient, sublimely indifferent to the clamor around us.

Want of time compels me to skip a portion of my story It is impossible to give all the details of our doings. You have seen how we started, and after we were fairly under way the work became in a measure uninteresting. Not that it lost interest to us, but that our days were passed very much as I have described, and, therefore, an account of them would be mere uninteresting repetition.

Three times a week our ancient horse, "Bonaparte" as we called him, carried our crops to market. Sometimes he had a large load, and at other times a lighter one, as our crops varied greatly in their time of ripening. The largest money return we received for a load was forty dollars, and the smallest six dollars. As one crop ceased to produce anything it was pulled up, the ground again prepared, and some other crop put in. In this way nearly all our land bore two heavy crops during the season. If we had not followed some such course we could not have obtained the result we did.

One cool October afternoon, while the leaves were falling from the trees, and a purple mist lay on the far-away hills, I went out about sundown to see the flame and gold spread over Mount Arenac, and to take a short walk over our now nearly empty farm. All our crops have matured save the fall cabbages and the cucumbers. All traces of the others have disappeared, and the greater part of the field presents about the same appearance that it did when we came here six months ago. As I walked along I could not fail to contrast the present time with those first days when we came here, tired and half-sick, and started with doubtful steps in an untried field. Now we were both well, strong, and contented; happy in each other's company, and in a position of comparative independence. We have settled the question, — Farming can be made to pay. Robert's health is now so well established that I suppose we shall soon return to the city; yet I shall be sorry to go. Life is quiet, but very pleasant here. We have made many new acquaintances. Comfort, our friend and neighbor, is a treasure in her way; the two Stamford girls are companions no one would despise, sensible, well educated, and altogether charming.

And now we must leave them all, and many others equally pleasant. How I wish we need not! I wonder if it is not possible to spend the winter here? If it were only summer always we could support ourselves with ease, and could stay as long as we desired. I wonder if Robert could not find employment of some kind in the village for a few months, and so bridge over the winter. There he is, standing by the gate, talking with Mr. Kempenfielder. I'll go and ask him. As I came up I found they were comparing notes on our crops.

"So your sass farm paid its way, did it?"

"Yes, it did more than that. It paid for the care of the place, our support, and a little more."

"Well, well, it's mor'n I'd thought. Did you sell all your stuff? You had a mighty pile of it any way. I never seen such crops raked off any land before. Specks it was the manure that did it. Did you sell everything you growed?"

"Everything."

"What! them cabbages standing there? Are they sold?"

"Yes, I sold them to the Railroad this morning. I suppose they use them among their laborers on the new branch.

They offered five cents a head for the lot, and I took it at once."

"Only five cents? That aint much."

"Not much for a single head; but when it comes to over six thousand heads it is quite a sum of money."

"Six thousand heads! Why, that's three hundred dollars for the lot."

"Exactly."

"Well, well, it do beat all I ever heard tell. I don't wonder your farm paid its way."

Just then Jack came along and handed my husband two letters. Robert opened one of them and began to read it eagerly. While so occupied the sound of approaching wheels broke on our ears, and a heavy travelling carriage drawn by a pair of black horses trotted gayly past our gate. I tried to discover who was in it, but there was such a cloud of dust that I could see nothing at all. Robert was more fortunate. He evidently saw and recognized the occupants; for, as the carriage swept by, he crushed the letter into his pocket, and to my infinite astonishment started on the full run after it, shouting, "Doctor! Doctor! hold on! hold on!"

After a short run he caught up with the carriage, and it stopped. A brief parley was held, and to my still further surprise the horses were turned round and the equipage came slowly back toward our gate. Robert had got in, and was talking excitedly with the people inside, whoever they were. Utterly forgetting Mr. Kempenfielder, I stepped into the street to see who had arrived. As the carriage drew up to the gate, the door was thrown open, and out stepped our friend and physician, — the doctor.

"Why, Mrs. Nelson! This is indeed a surprise and a pleasure. I need not ask how you are. I have *prima facie* evidence of your health before my eyes. And your husband too. I did not know him; he is altogether a new man."

Before I could answer a word Robert jumped out, and assisting a lady to alight brought her to me.

"Julia," said the doctor, "this is Mrs. Nelson, another of my patients. Mr. and Mrs. Nelson are the two young people I told you about. You remember I sent them into the country last spring when they were both nearly dead."

"Indeed, doctor, I did not know I was your patient before," said I, extending my hand to the pleasant little woman before me. "I am glad to see you, madam. Come in, both of you."

"Here, here, Nelson, what are you doing with those horses?"

"Going to put them in the barn."

"Oh! no; we can stop but a few moments."

"Cannot stop! But you must. Come, let me put them up while you stay to tea, or stay all night, or stay a week, — which ever you like."

"Really, Nelson, we must not. We have no time."

"Now, doctor, just listen to me. The last time I saw you, you gave me a prescription. I took it. It saved my life, as you see."

"Should say it did."

"Yes; and if you imagine I am going to let you pass my door, and not come in and make us a visit, you are gloriously mistaken."

Thereupon he led the horses away toward the barn, leaving the doctor and his wife to me. I at once took the cue from my husband's actions, and literally dragged them into the yard.

"Wait a bit, Mrs. Nelson. Don't be in such a hurry. We must stop and see your view. Come, Julia, let us sit down on the door-step and admire. Is it not a lovely prospect?"

"Lovely does not express it. It is grand."

Finding they were making themselves quite at home on our door-step, I sat down myself beside them. After gazing about for a few moments, the doctor's wife broke silence, —

"What river is that we see far down the valley?"

"The Hoosensacken."

"And the village?"

"Arenac."

"And the flame-and-gold-colored mountain beyond?"

"Mt. Arenac."

"Well, it is lovely, — it is more than lovely, it is grand. How is it you happened to come to such a charming spot?"

"We not only came to the spot, but it came to us."

"How so?" asked the doctor.

Just then my husband came up.

"Here, Nelson, tell us all about this. How did you happen to light on this charming place? When did you find it, and what have you been doing since I saw you last?"

"My uncle left it to us. We came here last spring, and have farmed it ever since."

"You don't say! I congratulate you; but I hope he left you plenty of money to carry it on. Farming does not pay as an investment."

"So I am told. Uncle Jacob did leave us a little money, but not enough to support us in idleness. We have both of us worked hard, and have earned a fair reward."

"In health."

"Yes; and in money too."

"Really, you surprise me. But then, I knew you would

succeed in anything if you put your mind to it. Come, tell us more about it. I am vastly interested."

"So I will, after supper."

If there is any one thing I pride myself upon it is my house-keeping. When it comes to getting up a supper, I shine. On this occasion I spread myself, and produced a marvel of art in its way, — simple, as became our rural home, but very, very nice. Our guests were delighted, and did ample justice to my skill. After tea Robert lighted a great, roaring wood fire on the hearth, and we all drew up to the cheerful blaze, for the evening was chilly. The doctor and his wife were all impatience to hear about our doings since our arrival in Arenac, and Robert soon gave them a detailed account of all our adventures, very much as I have told you, since we left the city.

"Now, tell us about the financial part. You say you made money by the operation. Give us the figures. They may aid me if I am ever called upon to give any one the same prescription I gave to you with such success."

"Come, Harriet, get out your ledger. You see, doctor, my wife was the clerk of the establishment, and kept the books."

The doctor's wife looked up surprised.

"Why did you do that? I thought your husband was a famous book-keeper."

"To save time. I could do it as well as he, and so leave him free to work on the farm."

"A very sensible plan," said the doctor.

Here we were startled by a knock at the door. On opening it, I was surprised to find our neighbor, Comfort Jones, on the step.

Here was a chance for a triumph, and I improved it. Our visitors, no doubt, had the usual city ideas of country people. Here was a pet sample of a country lady, and I paraded her before their astonished eyes with an immense deal of satisfaction. They were captivated at once. They had never met a more charming old lady, they said, after she had gone. Robert offered a seat, and, after being introduced, Mrs. Jones sat down with us before the fire, and our circle was complete.

"We were about giving our city-friends some account of our doings since we turned market-gardeners. I suppose you have no objection to hearing it also."

"Objection! Oh, no! nothing would afford me greater pleasure. It is the very thing of all others I should like to hear about. I should like especially to hear if it is true that you made money by your farm. Some seem to think you did, and others say it is not possible to make anything out of so small a place."

"The very point I was trying to get at," said the doctor.

So I got out my ledger, and Robert opened it to read such portions as would interest our company.

"In the first place," said he, "I will give you a list of our crops, and what we received for each, and then I will show you some of the bills. You can then compare the two, and see the result for yourselves. The first thing we tried was early peas. We planted half an acre of the 'Daniel O'Rourke' variety. We sold ten barrels at five dollars, and ten at four dollars each, which produced just ninety dollars for the crop. After they were gone we cleaned up the ground and planted it with fall cabbages; but I will tell you more about them soon."

"Planted two crops on the same land?" asked the doctor.

"To be sure. That is the only way in which to make money."

"Well, I never heard of that before."

"It is the common practice among our best market-gardeners," said Mrs. Jones.

"But how can they do it? Does it not exhaust the land at a fearful rate?"

"So it would if they did not spend money on it at an equally fearful rate."

"That is just the point. It costs so much to do these things, I don't wonder it does not pay."

"Wait a moment, doctor. Let me read a few pages more. Next we planted a half acre of 'Early Flat Dutch Turnips.' We laid out the money on the land in the form of manure 'at a fearful rate,' and the result was, to those who had to pull and tie them for market, simply 'fearful.' I never saw so many turnips in my life. There were upwards of thirty-five thousand roots. They brought us an average price of three quarters of a cent apiece, which amounted in the aggregate to two hundred and seventy dollars."

"Only three quarters of a cent?" said Mrs. Doctor. "Why, we have to pay a shilling a bunch in town, which would be four cents apiece. Somebody must make a profit out of it, if you don't."

"Yes," said my husband, "the jobbers and retailers do make a large profit out of it; but then they have all the risk and we have none. We sell at once, and for cash, whereas they have to run all the risk of finding purchasers, or having the goods spoil on their hands. The price paid to the grower seems small, but he is insured, and the insurance is worth something."

"Insurance is worth a great deal," said the doctor.

"Then we attempted to grow an acre of Tennisball and Curled Silesia Lettuce, but could not compass it. We only had thirteen thousand heads in all. We received four cents a head for the first thousand, which amounted to forty dollars, and two cents for the next two thousand, which gave another forty dollars; lastly, we sold eight thousand at one cent each, which gave us eighty dollars more, making in all one hundred and sixty dollars for our lettuce. The rest we lost through ignorance. We let them stand too long, and they went to seed on our hands. Among other things we forced a lot of potatoes, and when the young plants were well started, we planted them out one rainy day. We had something over seven hundred hills; they came in early, and brought a great price. The gross amount was one hundred and ten dollars. To economize room we sowed seed of the 'New Perpetual Spinage Beets' between the potatoes, and harvested sixteen bushels of nice greens, which brought about fifty cents a bushel, or eight dollars for the lot."

"That was not a very large crop, Nelson."

"No; but you see we got it from land that otherwise would have been idle; besides it only cost the labor and seed, which I suppose amounted to about one dollar. That reminds me of our radish speculation. At my wife's suggestion we planted radishes between the rows of lettuce."

"It was not my idea," said I; "I got it from the books."

"A very sensible plan, Mrs. Nelson," said the doctor. "A few books well read will put one well along on almost any road."

"As far as I can discover," remarked Mrs. Jones, "they got all their ideas from books."

"Oh! no, not all. If we had followed the books alone, and not used common sense and some out-door practice, we should have failed miserably."

"And yet," said the doctor, "without book I fancy you would have accomplished but little. It was evidently books, brains, and — "

"Yes; books, labor, and brains carried you through."

"Their case," said Mrs. Jones, "reminds me of Sir Joshua Reynolds' apt reply when asked what he mixed his colors with: 'With brains, sir.'"

"You flatter us, Mistress Comfort."

"Comfort! — What a pretty name!"

"Come, Julia, don't run off on a side-track. Let us stick to the turnips and lettuce. Now Nelson, we are ready to hear more. It is wonderfully interesting, — as good as a novel."

"Better than most novels," remarked Comfort; "for it is all real."

"Yes," said I, coming to the defence of the doctor's wife. "Comfort is a nice name, and becomes the wearer, for she is a dear, comfortable body as ever you met."

"Please, Mr. Nelson, give us more lettuce and some cucumbers. I need something cool after that."

"You shall have it, Mrs. Jones. We'll take up the cucumbers next. After the turnips were pulled up, the ground was covered with cucumbers. In order to do this we pulled up a turnip or two every six feet, and planted a few cucumber-seeds in the empty space. By the time the turnips were ripe the young vines were a foot long, and ready to spread over the ground. By so doing we lost a few turnips, but gained three weeks in time, and made one crop overlap another. The squash-bugs and other destructive insects troubled us greatly; but we showered the vines every morning with wood-ashes and plaster, and so fought the bugs off."

"Yes," said the doctor's wife; "but where did you find out that plaster would keep off the insects?"

"Harriet read it in one of our agricultural papers, —'The Country Gentleman,' I think. Our cucumbers gave us more trouble than any other one crop. Part of them we sold fresh, but the bulk of them went for pickles. The number of young cucumbers we had was something enormous,— seventy thousand, if I remember rightly. The cash return was one hundred and five dollars."

"But was it not a great job to gather them, Nelson?"

"It was, to be sure; but we employed girls to help us."

"Employed girls!"

"Certainly. They made the very best of pickers and helped us greatly."

"And helped themselves too, to money, and health, which is worth more than money."

"They did that, I can assure you. They were perfect little giants when they left us."

"It was a capital idea, Nelson. I have lots of girls among my patients who are always ailing slightly. A few weeks of out-door work on such a place as this would set them up for life. But, bless me, it would never do. It is not genteel to work."

"Just what the people about here said," remarked Mrs. Jones. "The mere fact that our friend employed a few girls in his market-garden created a small tempest among the villagers. They, too, thought it not genteel, etc."

"Great geese, all of them."

"Just my idea."

"Now, Nelson, go on, please. Let us hear more."

"To have a variety, we planted a half acre of the 'Early Yellow Six-Weeks Beans.' They did very well. We had about seventy-five bushels, which brought an average price of one dollar and twenty-five cents a bushel, which netted us just one hundred dollars. Lastly, we planted cabbages where the peas, beans, lettuce, and potatoes had been growing, and, after allowing a liberal margin for those that never came to maturity, we harvested seven thousand heads, and sold them all out in one lot for three hundred and fifty dollars. Wait a moment; there is one thing I did not notice, radishes."

"Just what I was going to remind you of," said I. I was proud of our radish speculation, and did not wish it forgotten.

"We planted radishes between our lettuce, and pulled and marketed it before the lettuce was incommoded."

"That is carrying things to a pretty fine point, Nelson. How much space did you have between the rows?"

"Twelve inches."

"Only a foot? I should call that farming by a foot-rule."

"Yes, ours was literally farming by inches. We had a very fair crop of radishes. We packed up and sold one hundred and five dozen bunches. They brought about seventy five cents a dozen bunches, or, in round numbers, seventy-eight dollars. Here is a list of all our crops, and the total amount received for them. It is from our balance sheet: —

Peas	$90 00
Turnips	270 00
Lettuce	160 00
Beets	8 00
Cucumbers	105 00
Beans	100 00

Potatoes	$110 00
Cabbages	350 00
Radishes	78 00
	$1,271 00"

"Now for the cost," said the doctor. "I'll warrant you it nearly came up to that."

Manure of all kinds . . .	$300 00
Labor of boy, six months . .	150 00
" " 2 girls, 30 days . .	90 00
" " 4 " 5 " . .	30 00
" " men and boys . .	24 00
Ploughing	32 00
Seed	10 00
Tools	15 00
Books	3 00
Interest on estate, six months .	36 00
Taxes	8 00
Team	50 00
Support of family . . .	420 00
	$1,168 00

"The grand total of cost is, as you see, one thousand one hundred and sixty-eight dollars."

"Just what I told you. I knew you would make little or nothing by your farm."

"I know it seems a very small profit, only one hundred and three dollars for all our labor; but you must bear in mind that our farm supported us both and paid the above profit. Now this is not the whole story; there are two more items to be entered. You must not think we sold our entire crop, and denied ourselves everything. We were not so foolish as that, I can assure you; we supplied our own table with the best our farm produced, and fairly revelled in fresh vegetables. To the amount of our sales must be added the value of the things used on our table. Then I sold our old horse and wagon for forty dollars, as we have no use for them in the winter. The account then stands somewhat in this wise: —

Received for crops . .	$1,271 00
Vegetables used in house . .	110 00
Sale of team	40 00
	$1,421 00
Expenses	1,168 00
	$253 00

"Our support and two hundred and fifty three dollars, — a little more than ten per cent. on the capital used. Our assets are as follows: Real estate, twelve hundred dollars; furniture and etc., three hundred dollars; tools, ten dollars; cash in Savings Bank, fourteen hundred dollars. Total, two thousand nine hundred and ten dollars. Debts none. A very satisfactory statement it seems to me."

"It may seem so to you, but for my part," said the doctor's wife, "I think you two people had to work pretty hard to earn the paltry sum of two hundred and fifty dollars."

"You forget, Julia, that they had their support from it, and made what is considered a fair profit, — ten per cent."

"Is that not the average return on capital invested in mercantile pursuits?" asked Comfort.

"Yes, most merchants are satisfied with that, and are willing to run every risk to obtain it. As far as I can understand it, Mr. Nelson was almost free from risk. His position was a safe one, as it was independent. No pressure in the money-market could affect him, for as long as people live they must eat. His market was assured to him as long as he chose to supply it. The only risks he does run are those of climate and competition."

"The first, doctor, all trades are liable to. The storm that throws down my corn may sink another man's ship, or blow over his tall chimney. As for the second, it would be an advantage to have another good gardener next door. We could help each other in various ways, and keep the market more evenly supplied, and, by selling cheap, create a market where none existed before. Besides all this, the non-producers, as a class, far outnumber the producers, and are likely to do so for a great many years to come. If our village of Arenac continues to grow as rapidly as it does now, ten years hence it will be a great manufacturing centre, and then a dozen such market-gardens as ours could not furnish the material that would be required to supply its market."

Just here Mrs. Jones rose, and, glancing at the clock, said: —

"Really, I must go. It is nearly ten; quite time I was on my way home. I am sure I am glad I happened in at so fortunate a moment. The account of your doings has greatly pleased me. I can but congratulate you on your success. I always supposed you would manage to get a living from your farm, and am truly glad you have done so much better than that."

Then she shook us each by the hand and bade us good-night. Robert offered to escort her home, but she declined, as the night was not very dark, and the road short; however, we all thought he had better go, and he went.

"What a pleasant lady your neighbor is! Have you any more like her?"

"Oh, yes! some of our rural friends and neighbors are very sensible, agreeable people."

"Well, Mrs. Nelson, all I can say is, I think your lines have fallen in pleasant places. I am very glad your husband saw and stopped us as we passed your gate. The story of your experience is one that will aid me, if I ever have a patient in the same position your husband was in last spring. What a change from your city home and life! Viewing your husband's illness from this distance, and in the light of its result, I am very glad he was sick."

"Really, doctor, that is a new view of sickness. I should not have been pleased to hear you give it last winter."

"Very likely. We never know what is best for us. Our blessings are generally disguised in some way."

"For my part," said the doctor's wife, "I fairly envy you, Mrs. Nelson. Such a charming home! You must enjoy life in this little box of a house. It must be a pleasure to take care of such a neat little place. Our great city house and retinue of servants are all very fine at a distance, but, as a home, yours is the best. You have no servants and but little care. We have plenty of both. Henry Ward Beecher once said, that 'A brown stone front was a means of grace.' He was more than half right."

"Besides," said the doctor, "Mr. and Mrs. Nelson have one other advantage over us city people; for they have proved that in their case, the old proverb is true, —'the happiest people live in the smallest houses.'"

Soon after this I lighted a candle and conducted our visitors to their room, as they had travelled a long distance that day and were very tired. At the door I bade them good-night.

CHAPTER VIII.

HEALTH, AS A FARM CROP.

CLOSING the door behind me, I procured a shawl, wrapped it round me, and sat down by the fire to wait and to think. Then I remembered how I had sat down just in this way once before. There was no need now of gazing at the embers in search of visions of the future. The time for dreaming had passed. A tangible reality was with me now, or would be soon. In a moment or two I heard it enter and with firm steps approach my chair. It sat down by my side, and then there were "four feet on a fender."

"A penny for your thoughts, Hattie."

"I was thinking of my dream."

"What dream?"

"The dream I had one night last winter, when I fell asleep by the fire while watching by your sick room."

"Oh! I remember. What a realization we have had of it!"

"Yes, indeed. It is almost startling so truly has it come to pass. Surely 'God has been a strong castle unto us.' He has saved you from the grave, and restored your health in a way that seems miraculous."

"It seems so, but is not. He helped us by showing a way in which we could help ourselves. He overstepped no laws to benefit us, but simply aided us, by pointing a road to health through obedience to sanitary laws."

"Well, any way, I am thankful."

"So am I, truly thankful. Thankful also that He has kept us together for another season, and given us a reasonable expectation of many years in each other's company, — leaving it a matter for ourselves to decide how long we shall live, within certain limits."

"How can that be?"

"You must admit that we both have good constitutions and are in perfect health at present."

"I do."

"And you see how the carrying out of sanitary measures placed our exhausted and debilitated frames in their present condition. Now, it is but fair to suppose that if we continue to follow the same sanitary rules, we can maintain the high standard of health we now enjoy for an indefinite time. That is, D. V., the Lord willing."

"Yes, but can we? Can we stay here any longer? 'The harvest now is over, the summer days are gone,' and we are not 'saved' — unless we stay here. That we cannot do."

"Why not?"

"Because you must return to Farwell & Co. We should

'quietly starve,' as you say, on the farm during the winter. It is true we have plenty of money in the Savings Bank, but we shall want it all to carry on our farming operations next summer."

The only reply I got to this was the unrolling of a crumpled piece of paper, — a letter it seemed: —

"OFFICE OF THE ARENAC PRINT WORKS,
October 10th.

"MR. ROBERT NELSON.

"DEAR SIR: Your application for the vacant clerkship in our office has been considered and accepted by the directors. They have decided to give you a salary of one hundred dollars a month, with the understanding that the engagement shall not continue over six months. At that time it is in contemplation to make some changes in the affairs of the corporation; therefore it is impossible to make any arrangements extending beyond that time. Your desk will be ready for you on and after the 15th inst.

"Respectfully yours,

"CHARLES JOBSON, *Agent.*"

"Now, isn't that perfectly splendid? Just what we wanted. Why, I almost want to kiss Mr. Dobson or Jobson, whoever he is."

"I would a great deal rather you would kiss somebody else." I did.

"Now, my dear, come close to me while I whisper a little secret in your ear."

"How can I? There is a limit to proximity."

"Did you know that our little farm produced one crop that, in money value, far exceeds all the rest combined, — in fact, a crop worth the sum of three thousand dollars?"

"Three thousand dollars!"

"Exactly."

"Really, my dear, I do not understand you at all."

"Do you remember how many times I tried when we lived in the city to get an insurance on my life?"

"Yes, I remember it with sorrow. No company was foolish enough to risk its money on such a precarious life as yours."

Just here I felt a curious movement as if something was being drawn forth from somebody's pocket. Looking up, I beheld before my astonished eyes a policy on my husband's life for three thousand dollars.

"There, Hattie, is our latest and best farm crop, — my health. The Arenac Mutual Insurance Company seem to think it so far restored that they value it at the above sum. It is in your favor. Allow me to present the policy to you."

"O Robert, Robert! This is too much happiness." And I kissed him, and kissed him, — but dear me, what am I saying? I have quite forgotten myself. This is a story about radishes and lettuce, not sentiment.

On the 15th of October, Robert burst his agricultural shell, mounted his high stool, shook his quill in the ink, and was — a book-keeper. As for me "I minded the house."

About the middle of the following February, it was given out that the Print Works had decided to build a new mill, that would give employment to six hundred hands. On hearing this my husband at once resigned his clerkship, and returned to the farm. If the six hundred new hands and their dependents came into the place, there would be at least one thousand more mouths to be filled. "Sass" would be in demand.

We began our farm work for the second year on the first of March by putting down a number of hot-beds filled with potato, tomato, cabbage, and lettuce-plants. As we had a larger capital to work with, our second year's sales exceeded the first. We spread the manure thicker, ploughed deeper, and cultivated still more carefully. The result was an income of twenty-one hundred dollars, which paid a profit of twelve per cent. on the investment.

The farm after this kept us fully employed all the year round with the exception of a few weeks in the dead of winter.

The third year we started with a cash capital of eighteen

hundred dollars; fifteen hundred of this was expended for manure. Perhaps you wonder at this. Many people imagine that one dressing is sufficient for several years. This is a great mistake. To compel the land to yield at the rate above mentioned, fertilizers must be ploughed or harrowed in every season, and in the most liberal quantities. The third year, at the suggestion of the market-man, we branched out and tried our hand at strawberries. We planted half an acre, after pulling a crop of early cabbages. It gave us one thousand boxes of berries the next year, which the market-man took at twenty cents a box, and would have taken more if we had only had them. After the berries were gone, the plants were ploughed up in time to plant dandelions for the next spring. You see we made our land give us an income at nearly all seasons of the year. Not an inch of the soil was suffered to remain idle a day, and every inch had to produce all that money, labor, and skill could wring out of it. Our sales the third year almost touched three thousand dollars, and have remained thereabouts ever since.

I wish I could tell you more of our doings. Want of time forbids a further extension of my story. My object in giving you this little sketch of our agricultural experience is to show you, or some one else situated as we were, a safe and profitable field where you can earn both health and bread, if you are so inclined.

Perhaps you reply, "This is all very fine, but is it true?"

"Yes, in its main features this is a true story of actual experience. The facts and figures I have given you are taken from accounts of bona-fide sales and expenditures of a real market-garden. The originals of most of the characters are still living in New England.

The question is often asked, Does farming pay? This is not a fair question. Does any business pay? Does boat-building, or soap-making, or carpentry pay? The question is not, Does farming pay, but, Can *you* make it pay? This is something I cannot answer, seeing I do not know you personally. I know nothing of your education or capabilities. Some men with the requisite skill and capital would make a fortune out of the manufacture of wooden clothes-pins. I could not. Whether you could or not is more than I know. If you had a son you designed to put into mercantile life, you would not ask, Does it pay, but, Will my son make a successful merchant?

More and more attention has been turned to farming of late years. Many are thinking of following the example of myself and husband. For them I have but one word: Be sure and farm

"WITH BRAINS, SIR."

www.ingramcontent.com/pod-product-compliance
Lightning Source LLC
LaVergne TN
LVHW021421110826
845150LV00007B/2025

* 9 7 8 1 4 2 5 5 0 8 4 5 6 *